STRONG WATER

TALES OF A MASTER SOMMELIER'S LIFE IN FOOD, WINE, AND RESTAURANTS

TIM GAISER, MS

Author's note: This is a work of creative nonfiction. While all the stories in this book are true, some names and identifying details have been changed to protect the privacy of the people involved.

ISBN: 978-1-959993-21-6

For Carla, Maria, and Patrick

CONTENTS

FOREWORD

Tim Gaiser and I first met during his journey to become a Master Sommelier in the 1990s. I served as one of Tim's examiners and had the delight of witnessing him navigate--and pass--the M.S. practical examination. In time, Tim would spend nine years as the Education Chair and Education Director for the Court of Master Sommeliers, Americas. His knowledge is comprehensive by anyone's measure. Tim is also a natural educator both in speaking and writing, and is able to condense info without robbing it of breadth and depth. Moreover, his wicked sense of humor is affectionate and appreciative, though never used as a weapon.

When Tim passed the MS exam in 1992, he was the 20th American to do so. There are now over 180. Tim once referred to our M.S. colleagues as "alpha-cats," and said herding them was challenging. "Strong Water" is a green room of sorts where all the alpha cats can relax and remember the irreverent, shocking, and hilarious truth about their work. Tim reminds us in the book, *"It's the restaurant business that never discriminates. It embraces one and all, no matter how dysfunctional or mutant the individual is. Everyone is equal in the eyes of the restaurant gods, and regardless of skill or experience, anyone can go down in flames. But one can also be a star."*

Tim wrote "Strong Water" for all of us in the food and wine business—his band of brothers who have spent our lives in wine and hospitality. These industries can forge amazing, incomparable fellowships—family, really. All born out of battlefield experiences in service, and in building the sommelier community in the U.S. pretty much from scratch.

The wine knowledge shared in "Strong Water" is a gift to both industry pros and consumers alike. Tim is a Master's Master, and one of our tasting gurus. His first book, "Message in the Bottle: A Guide to Tasting Wine," was intended for those we affectionately call "Jedi knights in training." But even if you're a newbie at tasting, "Strong Water" gives you an utterly accessible immersion into wine terminology, which Tim calls *"one of life's most delightful, shared hallucinations."*

When I'm listening to Tim talk about wine, I often find myself rapidly taking notes to elevate my own skills. If you're an enthusiastic wine consumer hoping for poetic descriptions, they'll come through like this one about a great Burgundy: *"The sum total shimmered like the surface of a quickly moving stream."* Then again, here's someone at the top of their game, without an ounce of ego bluster: *"Box wines, jug wines, canned wines, and wines in Tetra Pack are all relevant and important to our industry."* Take note, budding specialists!

"Strong Water" not only commemorates formative experiences with wine, but also celebrates Tim's appreciation of family, music, and food. Tim's deep love of family is a theme throughout, radiating authenticity and heart. The book is peppered with references to Carla, Maria, and Patrick, his beloved wife, daughter, and son. Wine and music are also inextricably linked for Tim, an accomplished musician who earned two degrees in music and played trumpet professionally before dipping into wine. *"Playing a musical instrument (or singing) requires immense focus. Tasting also requires great focus and the ability to shut the world out in order to discover what's in the glass."*

"Strong Water" comes from the wit and memory of a deeply accomplished person who's willing to share. And like watching any true professional, Tim makes it look easy. This book is a brightly lit bridge between those of us who earn our living in wine and hospitality and consumers. Thanks for bringing us together, Tim, over food, wine, and restaurants. I'm happy and proud to call you a friend.

Madeline Triffon, MS – August 2024

INTRODUCTION

I never set out to be a writer. Like everything else in my career, it developed through happenstance and a series of sideways moves. My initial attempts at writing were keeping journals on trips as far back as 1987, when my wife Carla and I went to Europe for the first time. Other journals followed with houseboat/fishing trips in the Sacramento Delta. In the mid-90s, I started to keep daily journals about trying to balance life working for a startup in Silicon Valley (Virtual Vineyards/the original wine.com) and raising two small kids in San Francisco. Needless to say, these scripts are valuable now, as so much of those early years with the kids are either a blur or completely forgotten. Time and beta blockers tend to obliterate all.

In April of 2001, I found myself unemployed, along with over 225 others who had previously worked at wine.com. I took the summer off to hang with my kids with the intention of finding a job in the fall. Then 9/11 happened, resulting in a freeze in wine industry hiring. At that point, I was forced to become an independent contractor, and I have remained so since that time. Over the years, my clients have included Champagne houses, wineries domestic and abroad, consorzios in Italy, Consejo Reguladors in Spain, and many more.

From 2003 through 2011, I was also the education chair/director for the Master Sommeliers in the U.S. What started as a part-time logistics job became full-time, leaving limited opportunity for writing. In early 2012, I was finally able to return to writing and start a blog. A majority of the content was about tasting and my tasting project. The intent was to write for several years and accumulate enough copy for a tasting book. Then, several years turned into ten.

Fast forward to March of 2020. After a last trip to Portland for an MS Advanced Exam, COVID-19 effectively shut everything down. Like countless others, I quarantined at home with Carla and my son Patrick and avoided the rest of the human race. But staying home was more than that for me. Because my career was olfactory-based, I all but hid under a couch for the better part of two years, even developing a sense of paranoia in the process when it came to crowds. To that point, several colleagues caught COVID early on. One of them had to leave the business after 20 years. He's just now getting his sense of smell back several years later.

The silver lining behind the very dark cloud of the pandemic was that it finally allowed me to finish my tasting book. In December 2022, I published *Message in the Bottle: A Guide to Tasting Wine*. The book is an in-depth resource of information needed to become a professional taster, and includes basic and advanced skills as well as an entire section of strategies for improving focus, smell, and taste memory.

The pandemic also created the impetus and time for me to write daily. Just months before, Carla gave me a one-year MasterClass subscription (an online education subscription platform) as a Christmas gift. The first class I watched was taught by Neil Gaiman, a favorite fiction writer. One of the many lessons I took from Gaiman's lectures was to simply carve out time every day to write, and that there was no substitute for writing on a regular basis.

I took Gaiman at his word and began to write what I called the "Daily 500," a short missive with a minimum of 500 words. The topic of each missive could be on anything, and the subject of the missives was infrequently on wine. Growing up in a big Catholic family in the 60s and going to parochial school provided more than enough fodder to begin this practice. Other 500 topics were about news of the day (grim at the beginning with the pandemic), the ever-turbulent state of politics, and complete and utter whimsy.

In time, 500 words became a thousand. In the last four years, I've written over a thousand of these missives. *Strong Water* is a sampling of them as they apply to food, wine, the restaurant business, and my days as a sommelier. I've also included wine trip experiences and other bits that I hope will be humorous and entertaining. With that, read on and enjoy.

PART ONE

RESTAURANTS

Over time, I've come to believe that there are two great equalizers in life: parenthood and the restaurant business. I'll leave parenthood for a future book. Otherwise, everyone should do a stint working in a restaurant, be it a KFC or The French Laundry. Working the floor or behind the bar are two of the most intense and direct customer service jobs there are. One has to learn how to survive—and hopefully thrive—under chaotic triage conditions that are the lunch and dinner rush. Then there is dealing with the public, an education unto itself.

I worked in restaurants periodically from the time I was 16 until I left the floor for good at age 38. In between, there were years spent bussing tables, washing dishes, waiting tables, bartending, and working as a sommelier. Several times I left the industry only to return when other jobs ended or when cash was short. That is the business. While Irving Berlin's song about the Statue of Liberty may say, "Give me your tired, your poor, your huddled masses yearning to breathe free," the restaurant business never discriminates. It embraces one and all, no matter how dysfunctional or mutant the individual is.

Part I of the book includes a smattering of restaurant experiences over the years, along with a couple of nightmares I had long after leaving the floor. As I say in one of the chapters, you may leave the business, but it never leaves you.

1

MY FIRST RESTAURANT JOB

My first job of any substance was bussing tables and washing dishes at the now long-defunct Biff's Pancake House in Albuquerque. The story begins in the summer of 1971, after I finished my sophomore year in high school. I was 16 at the time, and the goal of working for "The Man" was to save enough coin to buy my first professional trumpet.

Truth be told, it wasn't my first job. That would have been the summer before when my older brother Tom and I chopped cotton for a week on my Grandma Wade's farm in South Texas. I'm not sure whose idea it was to enlist the two of us for five days of forced labor. Regardless, we earned a whopping $12 a day and $60 for the week. And we also got a wicked farmer's tan.

Even though $60 seemed like a windfall at the time, it didn't begin to cover the cost of a new trumpet. Any pitch I made for the parents to help me buy a new instrument—which would have cost between $500 and $600--failed to launch. They simply didn't have the money. After school let out in May of the following year, I got the job at Biff's. But there was a catch. The hours were Wednesday through Saturday, 6:00

PM to 4:00 AM. That's right, you heard it right. Ten-hour shifts for four consecutive days.

It goes without saying that this kind of nonsense wouldn't legally be tolerated now. Today, the state labor board would slap the owners of the restaurant sideways into tomorrow if they caught wind of anything resembling such skewed scheduling practices. But this was 1971, and indentured pancake servitude was the norm.

The restaurant's manager was a woman named Darla. She was a skinny, hard-edged, aging cowgirl who looked like she'd seen a lot of bad pavement. She was a chain smoker who kept a lit cigarette in hand, sometimes even during service. Darla also had a serious case of helmet hair styled with enough Aqua Net to waterproof a dinghy. The finishing touches were enough cake makeup to fill in a dented fender and a force field of some cheap, screeching floral perfume. The sum total was that Darla looked like Tammy Wynette's evil twin. But she was an absolute shark in the restaurant, barking orders to the staff in both the front and the back of the house.

The waitresses were all "lifers," older women who had worked at the restaurant for years. They constantly bitched about their tips, their feet, and Darla. At first, they treated me like a mutt some relative had suddenly foisted on them. But in short order, they discovered I could make their life at Biff's much easier. And that, dear friends, was because everything about bussing tables was squarely in my wheelhouse.

The very definition of the job required speed, repetition, and thorough-ness—all capabilities I had in excess. But there was one more critical element. After the first couple of shifts, I realized I had "restaurant eyes," a sixth sense of sorts that meant I could walk through a section of the restaurant and instantly see what needed to be done for any table at that moment. Restaurant eyes are a particular kind of peripheral vision required for one to have any success in the business. If you don't have them, you shouldn't even think of waiting tables, bussing, or bartending because the job will be hell for you. And you will probably suck at it. To this day, I can walk through a restaurant and see everything that needs doing. It's a curse.

I also discovered I could easily keep at least a half-dozen things in mind that needed to be done in the next few minutes. More importantly, I could prioritize them by whatever needed to be done first. My list constantly changed, with things done being removed and things needing to be done continually added. Finally, my recipe for bussing success included the fact that I was a skinny piece of sushi who could move fast. More often than not, I found myself refilling coffee or water because I was out of things to do in the moment. Thus, in no time, the aging wrecking crew of waitresses, who just days before would have taken me to the vet for neutering and de-worming without a second thought, adopted me as their idiot bastard son.

Once the gig at Biff's was secured, it was a matter of figuring out the commute. Getting there was no problem. I could ride the aging green Murray ten-speed bike that Mom and Dad had given me some years before. The jaunt was less than 4.5 miles (or so Google tells me). I could stick to riding on neighborhood streets for most of it. But the last stretch had me riding on the always-busy Wyoming Blvd. to cross over the freeway. The ride took less than 20 minutes, and I usually arrived sweaty but ready for a ten-hour shift.

Getting home after finishing up at 4:00 AM, however, was another matter. For the first week or so, my Dad insisted on picking me up, bike and all. Martin was 48 at the time, and the last thing he wanted to do was get up at 3:30 in the morning and drive anywhere, much less retrieve me. After a short time, I convinced him it would be OK for me to ride my bike home. And frankly, it was. I don't recall any incident ever happening other than being chased by random stray dogs. I also marvel at the fact that I was never stopped by a police car. I chalk it all up to luck.

Like many 24-hour restaurants, Biff's was a cross between a chameleon and a community theater for aliens at the edge of the universe. That is to say, its personality changed multiple times throughout the course of a day. At breakfast, it was a greasy hash-slinging pancake-waffle joint serving meals at light speed. That would change only slightly at lunch when regulars, who worked at nearby offices, had less than an hour to hoover sandwiches and the like.

Dinner was the slowest meal service of the day. Fortunately, the restaurant's location helped, as it was on Central Avenue, part of the old Route 66 that traversed the entire length of the city. A good deal of dinner business was made up of hungry tourists passing through Albuquerque who did not want to wait until Clines Corners on the other side of the mountains or the remotely distant Tucumcari to stop.

Then there were the tour buses. Many times, one or more buses pulled up in front of the restaurant filled with Southern Baptists headed to a convention somewhere in the Deep South or with army guys headed to a base in Texas. Then, it was all hands on deck as half of the restaurant would get seated in short order. In minutes, the place would get slammed. First, the waitresses would be overwhelmed, and then the kitchen would groan and creak under the weight of getting 20 or more orders at once.

During tour bus times I would take on the role of rabid chihuahua busser, moving as fast as I could and trying to cover drinks, get sides, and clear plates as needed--along with the usual refilling of coffee, sodas, and water. In no time, the checks would be paid, and the hordes would reboard their buses bound for highway glory. Then, the real work would begin with a massive cleanup and resetting of tables, not to mention attending to the restrooms. Yes, at Biff's the busboys had to monitor the restrooms during their shift—even the ladies' room. I got my first taste of cleaning public restrooms there, a curse that would follow me into college when I was a janitor at a church for the better part of three years. Suffice it to say that, to this day, I abhor cleaning toilets.

If breakfast, lunch, and dinner were the first three acts of a psycho-waffle drama, the post-bar rush that started shortly after 1:30 AM was a bizarre Fellini-esque finale where the babysitter turns into an evil clown, the aging priest disappears with all the potted plants, and the tragic anti-hero is pulled down to hell by a commendatore dressed in drag.

The cruel irony was that the busiest—and craziest—part of the 10-hour shift happened after I'd been on my feet for almost eight hours. As soon as the clock struck 1:30, all the bars that dotted Central Avenue would start to give last call. Within minutes, the restaurant would be crammed to the gills with denizens of the drink in every shape, size, and persuasion: sloppy businessmen, guys on a rowdy night out, frat boys, prostitutes, and more. The noise was deafening, and the cigarette and cigar smoke was thick. No surprise that after a night of boozing, everyone was famished, and people wanted their steak and eggs, omelets, and strawberry pancakes *right now*.

Months later, when school started back up and my schedule was relegated to weekend mornings, I experienced the breakneck pace of breakfast service with its own flavor of triage. The post-bar rush was all that and more because of the chaos created by a bunch of drunk, unruly customers. The amount of coffee I poured was astonishing. I could barely keep ahead of demand by brewing fresh pots. "These people are drunk," I would think. "What the hell is all this coffee going to do?" In reality, the coffee served to create a much-needed buzz and metabolic momentum that would last just long enough for people to eat and then drive home, hopefully without getting into an accident.

10-17-21

2

RED AND LITTLE BUD

Two regulars of the bar rush crowd at Uncle Biff's stand out in memory. First, a creepy, ruddy-faced guy who I came to call Red. He always wore expensive suits and was accompanied by three or four young guys. At first, he was overly polite with me, offering profuse thanks any time I cleared a plate or refilled his coffee. Then, after seeing him a few times, he kept me at the table to chat me up. "They don't appreciate how good your work is here. They probably don't pay you enough, either. I can offer you a job that's much easier and will pay twice as much." I thanked him but didn't say more. After all, it's not every day you get offered a job at 2:00 A.M. "Meet me on such-and-such corner on Monday afternoon at 3:00," he said, "I'll tell you about the job then." I murmured some kind of answer but never went back to the table.

The next day, I told my Mom about Red and his job offer. "He sounds like a criminal, and the last thing you should do is meet up with him," she said. I didn't know about the criminal part, but I agreed with her about skipping the meeting. As always, her advice was spot-on, and I didn't give it another thought.

It was only a matter of time before Red made another appearance at the restaurant. When I approached the table to pour coffee, he berated me, saying, "Where the hell were you? Why didn't you show up?" I explained that my Mom thought he was a criminal. Actually, I just told him I was happy with the current job and wasn't looking for anything. Then I scooted away from the table before he could say anything else. But every time I looked his way, Red glared at me and gave me the evil eye, as did the young guys who were with him.

When I was leaving the restaurant that night, I asked one of the cooks, a burly guy who'd just finished a stint in the Navy, to walk outside with me to make sure Red and the boys weren't waiting. Fortunately, the parking lot was empty. That was the last time I saw Red and his entourage. God only knows what he did. My sense, like my Mom's, was that he was into dealing drugs, stolen cars, or something even more unsavory.

Then there was Little Bud. By day, he was a mechanic. By weekend night, he raced cars on a dirt track. More than anything, Little Bud was a large mutant slob of a human being with just enough intelligence to be annoying and/or dangerous. He was also a stereotypical bully who surrounded himself with several miscreants who were even bigger losers. But Little Bud was also Darla's nephew, so he could do no wrong.

I only saw Little Bud and his gang after he raced on Friday and Saturday nights—and after they had had too much cheap beer. Then Little Bud would come in, dirty racing gear and all, and hold court with his slackers at a large booth at the back of the restaurant. Approaching the table was dicey, to say the least. Pouring coffee was met with insults, jeers, and crumpled paper napkins bouncing off the side of your head. All the while, Little Bud, covered in dried sweat and smears of grease, laughed like a donkey, showing off two missing front teeth.

I quickly adapted the boxing strategy "stick and move" whenever I had to deal with Little Bud's table. This meant I would approach quickly while most of them were distracted, get done what I had to as fast as possible, and then get the hell away from the table. It usually worked—but not always.

I thought I'd seen the last of Little Bud when I moved to weekend breakfast shifts a few months later. Sadly, not the case. While washing dishes one Sunday morning, I heard the familiar donkey laugh outside the restaurant. "Dear God, please don't let that idiot back here," I silently pleaded. But God must have been busy with the church thing, it being Sunday morning and all. Minutes later, Little Bud's ugly, toothless mug made its appearance. At that moment, the other dishwasher and I were in the middle of cracking hundreds of eggs into a huge metal bowl that would be ferried to the cooks to make omelets.

After uttering several unintelligible insults, Little Bud spotted the tall stack of full egg cartons. Instantly, he grabbed eggs in both hands and started flinging them at us, laughing hysterically. We had no recourse but to run out the back kitchen door in defense, only to have Little Bud go tell Darla we were screwing around on the job. She immediately found us and read us the riot act, saying we would be fired the next time it happened. We tried to tell her what happened, but she refused to listen. I silently cursed her helmet hair--and Little Bud's dumbass mug, too.

I wasn't long for Biff's after the egg incident. By then, I'd saved enough money to buy a trumpet, and I was also getting too busy with school. But the place, with its brutal hours and nutty cast of characters, was the quintessential first restaurant job. The job where you learn if you are wired to work the floor and if you can even hack the gig. During my stint there, I discovered that I had restaurant eyes and could move quickly. As much as anything, bussing tables at Biff's taught me how to store, prioritize, and efficiently accomplish multiple tasks on the fly; something that continued to benefit me in every future restaurant gig and beyond.

As for Biff's, it closed down many years later, and the building was razed. But I still have plenty of janky memories of the joint. It reminds me that everyone is equal in the eyes of the restaurant gods, and that regardless of skill or experience, anyone can go down in flames. But one can also be a star, especially between the hours of 6:00 PM and 4:00 AM on weekends.

10-19-21

3

RESTAURANT NIGHTMARE
NO. 1

Working in the restaurant business for any length of time will inevitably lead to nightmares. One of the common themes is being in the weeds—overwhelmed--to the extent that there is no hope for survival, much less recovery. However, one of my restaurant nightmares morphed into something far more sinister with the addition of all my trumpet-playing angst.

The setting for the dream was Bix restaurant in San Francisco, where I bartended from the summer of 1988 to the end of 1990. The scene was a repeat of the very first Labor Day Sunday night I worked solo behind the bar. We had only been open for a couple of months at the time, and the press—all very positive—had started to reach critical mass. Add to that the fact that it was a holiday weekend with a lot of people in the City, and we were only staffed for a usual Sunday night. The stage is now set.

The dream took full advantage of what was one of the worst bar shifts I ever experienced. Mind you, at the time, I was a fast service bartender who could keep up with just about anything. I could get weeded, but rarely would I ever be overwhelmed. The dream itself started with another bartender and me having a pre-shift Fernet behind the bar, as per usual. Things started slowly, and everything was just ducky. But in no time, we were slammed with a tsunami of people, and both of us were soon completely screwed.

In the middle of it all, a rerun of the actual disastrous Labor Day night from 1988 was taking place. A couple sitting at the bar ordered a bottle of expensive Champagne from me. I think it was a bottle of Taittinger Comtes de Champagne. I quickly opened and served it to them, and then put the bottle in my ice at the service end. Afterward, I raced off trying to put out various fires while the service register printer was out of control, spitting out cocktail tickets like a cartoon.

At some point, I went to pour more Champagne for the couple, but I found that the bottle was gone. I had a moment of utter panic thinking I had poured off the rest of the bottle for an order for cheap sparkling wine by the glass. I stood there stunned, like in one of those wildlife movies where a wildebeest is at the watering hole. Suddenly, a croc-odile the size of a Buick rises out of the water and takes it down. At that moment, I looked down to the end of the bar, where the other bartender was also about to go under for the last time. Then he raced up to me and said, "Aren't you supposed to go on now? Don't you have to play?" I looked at him, completely mystified.

Instead of answering, he pointed to the backbar which had somehow transformed into huge floor-to-ceiling black curtains. When I found the part in the curtains and opened it, there was a stage with an audience of hundreds all staring at me. Then, I looked over to see a woman in a formal black dress seated at a grand piano. She was glaring at me and pointing to her watch. Next to the piano was a stand with music and a chair with my C-trumpet on it.

I walked over to the stand, much like the aforementioned wildebeest, and picked up my horn. Suddenly, I saw that there was no mouthpiece in my trumpet. And the music on the stand was the Tomasi Concerto, a hideously difficult piece I'd tried to play as a grad student but could never pull off. Then I realized I hadn't touched the horn for over six months (in real life, it was more like a decade). How could I possibly pull this off? I looked out at the audience and then back at the woman at the piano. The silence was menacing. At this point, I woke up in a sweat, and my heart was pounding. What the hell.

2-19-20

4

RAT TALES

After moving to San Francisco in the fall of 1984, Carla and I both applied for the same bartending job at Scott's Seafood on Lombard Street. She got the job and worked at Scott's until they closed in the late 90s. I spent the next few months pounding the pavement, trying in vain to get a bartending gig. At the time, getting a decent restaurant job in the City was a classic Catch-22 scenario. To get a job, one had to show proof of previous experience at a place in town. But how do you get that all-important first gig if you can't show previous experience? All of which meant that I was given a polite but firm *nyet* at dozens of places where I applied.

After the holidays, money was getting tight. One Friday afternoon in early January, I was walking up and down Union Street, putting in applications and trying to talk to bar managers. Note to self, never call on anyone in a restaurant on Friday afternoon. Unless it's a joint about ready to permanently shutter, the entire staff of any decent place is battening down the hatches for a busy weekend. The last thing they want to do is talk to anyone about a job. That's an activity reserved for

Tuesday through Thursday, a rule I also learned to follow when selling wine some years later.

Toward the end of the day, I found myself standing in front of an Indian restaurant called Assam. I paused momentarily before walking away. In hindsight, I should have kept walking. After all, it was late Friday afternoon, and our apartment was less than 15 minutes away. But I didn't. Instead, I went back and entered the place, only to discover a dimly lit bar with a stage and set up for a band.

An older bespectacled gent behind the bar introduced himself as George and asked if he could be of assistance. I told him I was looking for a bartending job. His eyes lit up. This should have been a warning, but I'd been looking for work for a couple of months. George quickly retrieved a job application and handed it to me. I took it to one of the dingy tables and filled it out in the half light. Then I handed it back to him. He scanned it, noting my MM degree and my experiences having worked in places in New Mexico and Michigan.

"When can you start?" he said suddenly.

"What?" I said, stunned.

"When can you start? We have an opening," he responded.

"I have applications at two other places with interviews lined up," I said. When in doubt, make things up. It's always been my motto.

"Why don't you come back tonight to hear the jazz? You can see the place in action," he said.

I told him I would. But even after applying to dozens of places, I didn't have the good sense to ask about pay, benefits, and schedule. I was too stunned at actually being offered a job.

I went home to tell Carla the good news. "What kind of place is it?" she said. "It's a dive jazz bar attached to an Indian restaurant," I told her. "Wow," she said, clearly impressed. Or alarmed.

We did go back that night and had a drink, which, if memory serves, was a cheap well Scotch on the rocks. The bar was full, and the jazz group was decent. George and his partner David both talked to me about working there. George quickly told me that the job was a cash-only situation with no benefits. The pay was $40 under the table per shift. However, the schedule was flexible, which meant that I could easily take time off to play trumpet gigs. There was one more thing. I would have to wear a short-sleeve safari jacket as part of the gig. At least it wasn't a clown suit.

Having no better options, I took the job and started the following weekend. In short order, I discovered that the place was somewhere between an island for misfit toys and a halfway house in another dimension. The clientele was a mix of hard-drinking types who clung to the bar for hours and jazz fans. Both were notoriously cheap and bad tippers. The cast of regulars belied description. Even though the memory of many of them has faded, some remain permanently engraved in my internal Etch-A-Sketch. Thank God I had the sense to write about the place during my tenure there.

I spent a long year working behind the bar at Assam, periodically submitting applications at other bars and restaurants. Meanwhile, life there was a nonstop Fellini-esque affair, serving a cast of regulars who were beyond a motley crew. Even though they came and went, one thing remained constant: the rats.

Most of the buildings on that part of Union Street were built in the 1880s and somehow survived the 1906 earthquake and fire. They were all three or four-story wooden structures built almost on top of each other. With buildings so old and so close together, rats had to be a problem. And they were.

The rare times I worked a day shift I had to report for duty at 11:00 AM. Business during the day was so slow that my job was to clean the bar, which was no small task. All the fixtures were in the latter stages of the putrefaction-decay cycle. The bottoms of the beer coolers were rusting. The slime in the drains could have been featured in *Plan Nine*

From Outer Space. But as tedious as the day shifts were, the first 15 minutes were always memorable.

When I first entered, the curtains were drawn, and most of the lights were off. Within seconds, I could hear a frenzy of scraping and bumping noises on the floor accompanied by high-pitched squeaks. I quickly retreated behind the bar to turn on a few lights. Within a few minutes, Mr. Patel, the restaurant owner, would join me.

Day shifts began with Mr. Patel offering a polite "good morning" and then getting down to business. In hand, he carried a hammer handle and a large garbage bag. First, Mr. Patel would turn on the rest of the lights to create a momentary glare. Immediately, a frenzy would break out on the bar floor and the band stage. Rats that had become stuck to glue traps during the night scurried about trying to escape.

Sometimes, up to a dozen would be cowering in various places, including under the permanently out-of-tune baby grand on the stage. Then Patel would track them down, one by one, and bash their brains out with the hammer handle before picking up the rat and trap combo and depositing it in the garbage bag. In a few short, violent minutes, the job would be done. Patel would then exit without saying another word, headed back to a large dumpster in the alley behind the building.

Mr. Patel probably viewed the daily de-ratting as part of his morning routine, much like folding napkins or polishing silver before a shift. Whatever the case, once he was finished, my day officially began.

4-20-22

5

GREAT ESCAPES

Beyond Mr. Patel's daily *Mad Max* routine, rats were a regular part of life at Assam. Not that the dining or drinking public knew about it. The city public health department would have frowned upon it. But all too often, a sudden screech could be heard from the dining room after an errant rodent dropped from one of the timbered rafters above onto someone's table in the middle of dinner. Then Mr. Patel would quickly be called out of the kitchen to triage the horrified and now far-from-hungry guests. Most demanded that the entire meal be comped. Mr. Patel, ever the scrupulous businessman, wouldn't budge beyond comping the drinks. A free meal was out of the question, rodents or not.

Beyond that, any movement out of the corner of one's eye wasn't imagined but was usually a scampering rat headed for the cover of darkness beneath a table or through an unseen crack in the ancient walls. Late at night, I'd often scan the timbers over the lounge area only to see a rat quietly prowling above.

I saw rats in the joint so many times it became routine. However, two particular incidents stand out. The first had to do with getting ice. It should be noted that the bar and the restaurant were separate businesses. Though it seems like a minor technicality, it caused headaches with bookkeeping and payment when food was ordered at the bar or in the lounge. But that was rarely a problem because the regulars who manned the bar stools weren't there for the comestibles—they had come for combustibles.

The ice machine was another matter. For whatever reason, Mr. Patel refused to let the bar personnel use the restaurant's ice machine, conveniently located just inside the kitchen door. On the other hand, the bar's ice machine was up on the third floor outside on a narrow stoop.

Needless to say, getting and restocking ice was a complete pain. Add to that the fact that I was the only bartender willing to go get ice at night during the middle of a shift. There was a good reason why. The rain gutters on the top of the two buildings were so close together that they were separated by an inch at most. But it was more than enough space for a host of rats to dangle their tails down in between. The effect was like seeing a row of skinny, hairy gray icicles in half-light.

At least once during a busy shift, I'd have to trek up three dimly lit flights of stairs, carrying an empty bucket and a large aluminum ice scoop. Once at the top, I'd unlock and open the door and then step outside to the ice machine. Next, I'd fill the ice bucket as quickly as I could using the ice scoop, and then set the bucket down just inside the door.

Then it was showtime. I'd quietly return to the ice machine, this time closely studying all the rat tails dangling down between the two gutters. I'd quickly select the largest and longest tail. Then, in what can only be described as a moment of utter recklessness, insanity, and stupidity, I'd take the aluminum ice scoop, reach up, and hit the longest rat tail as hard as I could, smashing it against the opposite rain gutter.

Instantly, all hell broke loose. A chorus of rat squeaks and squeals erupted, most notably from the victim whose tail I had just permanently maimed. An explosion of scampering noises followed. I didn't stick around to find out what happened next. Instead, I leapt inside and slammed the door shut as quickly as possible, locking it. Then I bounded down the stairs with ice bucket and scoop in hand.

Downstairs the chaos of the bar scene continued unabated in my absence. I quickly filled both ice bins and then went back to slinging drinks and emptying ashtrays as if nothing had happened. No one was the wiser about my game of rat tail roulette just moments before, which was definitely for the better.

Otherwise, much to George and David's credit, Assam was one of the few places in the City where one could hear live jazz seven nights a week. The featured groups were trios or quartets of local talent. Most were quite good. The music started at 8:30 with the banda du jour playing four 45-minute sets, finishing up just before 1:00 AM. Typically, things were really busy during the second and third sets when the place filled up. Then a lot of cocktails had to be slung in short order. But the action tapered off once the last set started, usually around midnight. It goes without saying that weekend nights were the busiest, with Sunday through Tuesday nights the slowest.

It was toward the end of one of these slow nights that the second rat incident of note took place. The band was in the middle of what would be their last tune. Everyone sitting at the bar had their backs to me and was listening to the music. Everyone except for one guy seated right in the middle of the bar, who had fallen asleep with his head resting on his arms. He'd drifted off during the song before. Had it been earlier, I would have woken him up. But it being the last tune of the night, I didn't bother. The noise of everyone making an exit in a few minutes and the lights coming up would wake him up. If not, I'd do the deed.

As the band played on, I stood leaning against the back bar with my arms folded. Sleeping guy was right in front of me. Suddenly, I detected motion at the edge of my peripheral vision to the left. I whipped my head around to see a fairly large rat that had just dropped down from one of the timbers above and was now crouched on the end of the bar. It looked right at me and then took off, scampering down the length of the bar at light speed, dodging cocktail glasses and ashtrays as it went. When it got to sleeping guy, it leapt over his head with the grace and agility of an Olympic dressage move. In mere seconds, it scampered to the other end of the bar and jumped off into the darkness. However, the rat must have lightly grazed sleeping guy as it jumped over him because he suddenly bolted upright with eyes wide open.

"What was that?!" he said, startled.

In a split second I decided that lying—not discretion—was the better part of valor.

"What was what?" I answered. "You were asleep."

"But didn't you see something?" he asked in earnest.

"I didn't see anything," I answered, "I was listening to the band."

He responded by putting his head down and going back to sleep. The entire thing took less than 15 seconds. Thankfully, no one witnessed the great rat bar top dash but me or there would have been chaos. After the fact, I decided to keep mum about the incident. Had I told George or David, I'm sure they would have reeled off dozens of rat stories, some more ominous and shocking than mine. Sometimes, it's best to just not know.

There would be numerous other rat sightings in the months to come before I left Assam for greener pastures. But that was the only time a rat made its way onto the bar. And that was a very good thing.

4-22-22

6

RESTAURANT NIGHTMARE
NO. 2

With the exception of lifers or owners, everyone who works in restaurants leaves at some point, often moving sideways into another career. However, the restaurant business never leaves you regardless of when you leave the floor, behind the bar, or in the kitchen. Periodically, it careens back into your sleeping and dreaming life in the form of restaurant nightmares. To that point, my last shift as a waiter was sometime in the summer of 1981, over 40 years ago. My last shift on the floor as a sommelier—and in any restaurant—was on March 31st, 1993—over 30 years ago. But I still have restaurant nightmares. The latest one woke me up at 3:40 in the morning, not long ago. It went something like this:

- The place: a fern bar that looked like Henry Africa's, a joint at Polk and Broadway in the City in the 80s which was about six blocks from our apartment on Lombard Street. The cast included the following.

- The bartender: a skinny guy with greased-back hair and a pencil mustache. I don't recall his name, so I'll call him Slim.
- A waitress: in her 40s and very high strung. I'll call her Shirley for reasons soon to be obvious.
- The manager: a large woman with short, dishwater blonde hair. She was wearing a loud floral print muumuu. I'll call her June.
- The cook: a large unkempt swarthy guy. He plays a very minor role so will remain unnamed.
- The plot: As with all dreams, much of the actual sequence quickly faded once I woke up. I'll just hit the highlights as I can remember them.

In the dream, it was a Sunday night, and the only staff working were the ones listed above. Otherwise, the place is huge. June has divided the entire dining floor into two stations—Shirley's and mine.

There was also a cocktail lounge. However, the cocktail waitress didn't show. June has decided that Shirley will be handling most of the diners. I will only be given two or three tables but will have to handle the cocktail business. I'm not happy about it and protest but to no avail.

The doors open and it's quiet at first. Then June starts seating tables in Shirley's section in multiples. In no time, she's in the weeds.

Then a group of about eight young women wander into the cocktail lounge wanting drinks. They look like college-age sorority types, all dressed up. One approaches the bar trying to order. Slim tells them that I will be taking care of them. Meanwhile, he's busy talking to two women at the bar, giving them his undivided attention.

I then get what will be my only two tables of the shift. Both are deuces, couples out for Sunday dinner. I approach the first table and the guy tells me they want a bottle of Clos du Bois Merlot. He pronounces it *close dew bwas* several times. I acknowledge the order, thinking I can get the bottle and open it within a couple of minutes. Then I go to the other table. They both order white Russians and a bowl of the soup of the day to start. I think the combination sounds questionable at best, but then head to the bar to place the order.

I tell Slim I need two white Russians. "We're out of Russians," he says with a straight face. "White Russians," I say, "you know, like Kahlua, vodka, and half and half?" "That's not a Russian," he says. "Don't you know what a Russian is?" Then he goes back to talking to the two women sitting at the bar.

At this point, one of the women in the sorority group comes up and says they want to order drinks right away. I look over to see that the group now numbers around 20. Some of them look like they can't be of legal drinking age. June steps up right at that moment and tells me that I better card everyone before serving them anything.

I nod and then head off to get the bottle of wine. I open the wine cabinet to find it filled with the same kind of wine. Thankfully, it's the Clos du Bois Merlot. Just as I grab a bottle, Shirley comes up to me, visibly shaken. "She's filled my section!" she wails. I look over and see that Shirley must have more than a dozen tables. "I'll try to help out," I tell her before racing off to the kitchen to get the bowl of soup.

As I head to the back of the restaurant, I see that it's now filled with people waiting for tables. Some of them are now in the kitchen actually eating the food at prep stations. The cook is going nuts, shouting and waving a knife.

I grab a soup bowl only to discover there are no soup spoons—and that the soup has been devoured by the marauding diners. In desperation, I look around for anything vaguely soup-like. I spot something that looks like Beef Stroganoff and then fill the bowl with it. The chef yells at me, asking what the hell I'm doing. I bolt through the doors dodging various people eating whatever they can find.

I grab a teaspoon at the wait station and then serve the soup to the guy at table two. "Hey, where's our drinks?" he says. "Coming right up," I respond. I then go to the first table to present the bottle of Merlot, only to discover I don't have my corkscrew. I excuse myself and then try to find Shirley to borrow hers.

Shirley is easy to spot. She's sitting at one of my empty tables, head down and crying. "Shirley, I need to use your corkscrew," I tell her. "I don't have one," she blubbers, "I forgot it at home. And I have too many tables!"

At that moment, I was accosted by one of the women in the sorority group. "Are you ever going to take our order? This place is the worst ever!" I looked over to see that the group now numbers around 30, and some of the girls look like they can't be older than 15.

Then June races up to me looking completely freaked out. "There are too many people! I've locked the front door!" I tell her that she can't do that because it's against the fire laws. She races off waving her hands in the air with the floral muumuu trailing in her wake.

From there, the dream/nightmare speeds up and gets more intense, with other things going wrong. Shirley throws her apron on the floor and leaves. Slim is nowhere to be found. June is hiding behind the front check in desk. I'm the only soldier left standing. My diners have left their tables and are now confronting me about missing cocktails and why I haven't taken their order. Several of the sorority girls are also in my face asking for drinks. I still can't find my corkscrew--which is what finally wakes me up in a cold sweat with my heart racing.

There are times when I wake up from a strange dream and try to go back into a semi-sleep state to fix things so the dream has a happy ending of sorts. Not this time. I rolled over, took a deep breath, and then started to piece the disaster together. And now you know what I can remember.

In the end, it is said that Morpheus, king of dreams, reigns supreme in the sleep world. What a cruel bastard he can sometimes be.

And I never found my corkscrew.

7-23-21

PART TWO

FOOD

It's sometimes said that there is a difference between eating to live and living to eat. For me, growing up in a household with five siblings, it was the former. Dinnertime at the Gaiser household was usually chaotic and a Darwinian affair requiring dexterity and cunning. We also lived in Albuquerque, where fine dining in the 1960s and 1970s was as remote as the Dog Star.

I didn't experience great food until I moved to Ann Arbor for grad school in the early 80s. Carla got a job bartending at the Earle restaurant, which would prove invaluable for multiple reasons. First, as a student, I could drink for free. Second, the Earle's menu at the time was cutting-edge and featured superbly prepared seasonal French and Italian regional cuisine as well as a wine list with over 800 entries. Sommelier/wine director Steve Goldberg ran an outstanding beverage program. In time, he would become my first wine mentor and was mainly responsible for my getting into the business.

It was at the Earle that Carla and I both crossed the line to "live to eat." From then on, quality food, cooking, and dining mattered. Sitting down to enjoy a meal with a bottle of wine became one of the most important parts of any day. It still is.

7

A CASE OF GRITTY CHICKEN

"The floor was greasy that day, my friends."

— ANON.

There's an old saying that goes something like this. Comedy is when you stub your toe. Tragedy is when I stub mine. The incident in the kitchen the other night was actually both. And it made Carla laugh. In fact, it caused her to get the no-breathers right when we sat down for dinner. That's a good thing, after all. One should periodically try to make one's partner laugh. Because if you're funny, maybe--just maybe--they will tolerate your otherwise boring ass for another day.

Otherwise, as a preamble to describing the incident in question, I was just re-emerging from home quarantine for the second time in more than two weeks after doing the COVID Paxlovid rebound. I was eager to fuss up some dinner, Carla having manned KP duty the entire time I was holed up in my office. Dinner would be boneless chicken thighs sauteed on the stove top and finished in the oven, accompanied by roasted potatoes, cherry tomatoes, and garlic. A salad would round things off. The vino would be a bottle of the just-released vintage of a favorite California Sauvignon Blanc.

The prep went without incident. The only hitch was my thinking pan, meaning I had to occasionally stop to remind myself what I was supposed to be doing. That's COVID brain for you. Yes, everything was going just ducky. The table was set, bubbly water was poured, and a small votive candle lit. Everything was in the oven, and the salad was ready to go. Then, like proverbial lightning, a major kitchen disaster struck.

When the timer on my phone went off, I opened the oven door, potholder in the other hand. The prime directive was to take the large skillet with the chicken out of the oven to check the temp. Two things before getting to the brief action sequence:

First, I always use a quick-read thermometer to ensure the chicken reaches the required minimum temperature of 160 degrees. Medium-rare may be OK for beef, but slightly pink chicken gives me the yeechies.

Second, the new fancy stainless steel pan Carla bought last year is heavy. One Sunday in January during the NFL playoffs I followed the instructions on how to cure the cooking surface to the letter, only for the pan to end up looking like overlapping Rorschach ink blots. It definitely didn't look anything like the picture, just like those damned sea monkeys.

Now to the incident. Rest assured that I've taken things out of a hot oven thousands of times. But this time was different. COVID brain must have interfered—or serious operator error. What happened next was this. Using the potholder, I grabbed the now very hot metal handle of the pan and removed it from the oven rack. But in microseconds, as I turned to put the pan on the stove top, I realized the entire palm of my hand wasn't covered by the potholder and was now registering all 375 degrees from the oven. Fire. Hot.

As noted earlier, the result was simultaneously tragic and comedic. I lost control of the pan just before getting it to the stovetop. Then, just as with car accidents, time seemed to be altered. It was like the movies directed by Sam Peckinpah, where everything goes into super-slow motion and all the cowboys get shot.

Instead of a rain of gunfire, I watched in horror as the fancy big sauté pan filled with our winner-winner chicken dinner and the melted butter/olive oil combo slowly fell from the sky and hit the parquet floor. On impact, it made a great noise, as they used to say in the bible. I reacted by doing my best "spider scares the dickens out of Little Miss Muffet" imitation by jumping back several feet, lest I get splattered by the hot oil. I also watched the chicken bounce a few times before finally settling on the floor.

At this point, an expletive or two was definitely merited. In the old days, I would have barked like a beleaguered sailor. But experience has taught me that hissing curse words is far more effective and satisfying. After all, it worked for Voldemort. Otherwise, I was somehow eerily calm. The damage had been done. Then I heard Carla calling out from her office. "Everything OK?" I responded with something along the lines of "yes, everything's great. And dinner just hit the deck."

Immediately, it occurred to me that the 10-second rule was now in effect, meaning that food dropped could only spend seconds on the floor. The only problem was that I had already spent those ten precious seconds staring at the scene of the accident and swearing. I wondered if there was such a thing as a 30-second rule. If not, there now was.

I finally roused my carcass into action, picking up the chicken with tongs and putting it on a plate. I gently and thoroughly wiped it with multiple paper towels to remove any unwanted floor detritus. I then used almost half a roll of paper towels to wipe up all the oil splattered on the floor. However, despite my efforts, the floor was still shiny and a bit slippety, as we used to say to my daughter Maria when she was a tot.

From there, it was plating dinner and calling the family to the table. Entering the kitchen, Carla took one look at the floor in front of the stove and then looked at me all wide-eyed. "Oh no!" she said. Then she got the giggles. By the time she sat down, she had the no-breathers. I laughed too. What the hell was I going to do? My son Patrick was flummoxed. I didn't bother to explain.

As for dinner, the chicken was fine—even tasty. But there were a couple of bites on the gritty side. Chalk those up to roughage. Beyond that, the good news was that I somehow avoided burning my hand. And I had survived the chicken catastrophe unharmed. Rest assured, I'll use the biggest-ass oven mitt we own the next time I reach for a hot pan in the oven. And if anyone would like the recipe for gritty chicken, I'm only too happy to share. It's called Chicken "Floorentine."

8-19-22

8

GRANDMA'S APPLESAUCE
CAKE

Many of my earliest memories from childhood, at least before we moved from the South Texas tropics to the high desert of New Mexico, are filled with images of my maternal Grandma Wade's farm. It was a sprawling 2,000-acre expanse of cotton fields that surrounded her house, several barns holding farm equipment, a machine shop, and multiple garages. A paved semi-circular driveway went around the house, linking to Farm Road 1 which led to the nearby village of La Villa, population 500. Towering ebony trees filled with nesting birds during the spring lined the drive. Just across from the drive from the house was Grandma's flower garden, a screen-enclosed sanctuary home to hundreds of exotic plants she had collected on her travels. Rumor had it that she had even been to Cuba at some point in the 1950s before the Castro era.

Several sizable corrals that once held cattle were just a stone's throw away from the house. By the time I was old enough to clamber over the fences, the corrals were covered in burlap and filled with acres of aloe vera plants that Grandma sold to a company that processed them for health and medicinal purposes. It is no surprise that she was a staunch believer in the healing properties of aloe. Every morning she slathered her skin in clear aloe vera gel until shiny, then applied a generous layer of Jungle Gardenia powder. Grandma even drank watered-down aloe gel for her digestive tract. She kept it in quart Mason jars in the fridge. Only problem was that she kept drinking water in the same kind of jars. Sometimes, I reached into the fridge for a jar of water to pour a tall glass, only to take a huge gulp and realize it was aloe. Ack!

Inside the house several refrigerated air units that were mounted in the windows continually hummed. Originally, Grandpa had central AC installed when the house was built, which was revolutionary for the time. However, after he passed, Grandma installed the window units because she didn't trust central air conditioning. With refrigerated air constantly on, a musty smell permeated the house. Enter the middle bedroom, stacked floor-to-ceiling with old newspapers and magazines, and the mustiness was like a force field. Yes, Grandma was a hoarder long before it became fashionable TV. As for the musty smell, only many years later would I learn that it was trichloroanisole—or TCA— the same compound that taints wine corks. And to think that I was inundated with it at times as a child.

At some point, Grandma started to use a single crutch to get around. The crutch also served as an instrument of discipline, often used to keep the mangy lot of us in line. Many times, a sudden whack across the butt would put an end to the tomfoolery of the moment. Then there was the time when Grandma caught my older sister Tina and me trying on her wigs in the bathroom. Many whacks were instantly issued.

When Grandma wasn't whacking us with her crutch, she was in the kitchen at the stove or the counter, prepping something for the next meal. My memories of Grandma's cooking involve a lot of breaded protein deep-fried in butter or lard. Vegetables from the multi-acre garden, just beyond the aloe corrals, were summarily shot on sight and then rendered into dark matter on the stove. Anything in the green vegetable universe was khaki by the time it was served. Boiled okra, one of Granny's favorites, had the texture (and color) of snot. When the okra was breaded with cornmeal and fried, it had a crunchy outer crust but still the same mucous inner layer.

Aside from deep-fried beast and khaki veggies, the true staple of Grandma's cooking was her applesauce cake. It was—and still is—the stuff of family culinary legend. I remember watching her standing at the counter, crutch at the ready, mixing the cake directly into an enormous rectangular baking pan. It goes without saying that Grandma didn't need a recipe, having previously made the cake from scratch hundreds of times. As she mixed up the batter, she talked non-stop in her raspy/whiny voice, telling me what ingredients were being flung into the pan at the moment.

Truth be told, cake assembly was so fast that it was hard to keep up. But the last step before putting the pan into the oven was the best. Then, to get all the air bubbles out of the batter, Grandma picked up the pan and dropped it back on the counter from a height of about 12 inches. It landed with a deafening smack. Granny did this repeatedly until she was satisfied that all the hidden bubbles in the batter were gone. To me, it was a thrilling moment of full-contact baking.

Some 45 minutes later, the cake was taken out of the oven and left to cool. Finally, after several preemptive cake strikes on the part of us kids had been warded off by the evil crutch, slices of warm, almost gooey cake were cut and served with ice cream. The first bite was beyond delicious.

In the first few years after we moved to New Mexico, Grandma would always visit bringing a cake in her luggage. It was a treat beyond compare. Grandma also taught Mom how to make her applesauce cake. But try as she might, Mom's version was never quite as good. I'm sure Albuquerque's high altitude and dry climate were to blame. However, I also have to think that Grandma was the source, urtext, and author of great applesauce cakes.

In the years since, I've never tasted another applesauce cake remotely as good as Grandma's. Her glorious applesauce cakes will live forever in my memory, along with cotton fields, ebony trees, and acres of aloe vera plants. And that's how it should be.

10-16-21

9

AL FRESCO

An online dictionary defines the title of this chapter as follows:

adverb

1. (especially with reference to eating) in the open air. "in the unlikely event of some sunshine, you can even dine al fresco"

adjective

1. done or eaten in the open air. "an al fresco supper"

If you live in San Francisco, there's a continental divide of sorts. Outside the City it's largely unknown, only familiar to residents, current and former. The divide is marked by the hill where the University of San Francisco is located and the nearby confluence of Geary Street and Masonic Avenue. There's a smallish shopping center at that intersection, the site of a former Sears, Best Buy, and other victims of ever-changing retail times. But if you stand in the parking lot there on practically any day, the cold and wet ocean wind will knife right through you, regardless of season.

East of the divide in the more spendy neighborhoods (which now, in reality, defines the entire City), the fog and clouds burn off much earlier in the day to create late morning sun, warmth, and semi-normal weather. West of the divide, it's a different story. The fog and clouds burn off in the early afternoon only to return several hours later. Or not. During the summer months, the marine layer, as the locals call it, can be so thick that it never recedes during the day. Sometimes for several days in a row. For the record, people in the City affectionately call the fog "Karl."

During the last 15 years that we were in San Francisco, we lived in the Sunset District, a cruel misnomer. If there is a foggiest part of the City, the Sunset is it. The odds of seeing an actual sunset, especially during the summer, are somewhere between slim and none. During those bleak, overcast, and cold summer months, we kept flannel sheets on the bed and wore fleeces indoors 24/7 while the rest of the planet sweltered in seasonal sun and heat. Mark Twain's alleged quote about the coldest winter he ever spent blah, blah, blah was--and still is--true.

It is no surprise that the possibility of enjoying a meal outside at the Pacheco Street manor was remote. In fact, during those 15 years, I can count on one hand the number of times we dined out back. The answer is zero. Yes, we never enjoyed a meal outside. However, we did sit on the front steps a few times when it was warm and enjoyed a cocktail. And we marveled at how one could be outside sipping a drink. What a concept.

Things are different now behind the adobe curtain in New Mexico. No more cold ocean fog nonsense. Now it's high desert and four seasons that go freeze, thaw, broil and marinate. For the record, I like marinate the best. It's spicier. Regardless, summer here always involves a week or two of brutal heat. Right now we're in the midst of that, with most days in the last two weeks reaching over 100 degrees. But things are changing. Just this afternoon it actually rained for the first time in over two months, bringing slightly cooler temps afterward. It's like Annette Funicello finally made an appearance at the beach in her new tankini. Bless her for that.

We'll soon have cooler temps and can venture out back for dinner. Then we'll do our best imitation of Marcello Mastriani and Anita Ekberg in Fellini's *La Dolce Vita* (above) and dine al fresco on the patio. Which means we'll tarry at the table long after the meal as the light fades. Do I need to say that it will be beyond grand? Memories of freezing in the not-so-sunny Sunset will seem like ancient history.

Al fresco. The Europeans had it down to a science long before we ever thought about roasting weenies at the park. They know that it's not just about being outside for a meal, it's the fact that you're there for a duration of time enjoying company, conversation, and more. To them, dinner is not about hoovering shrink-wrapped goodies or take-out in front of the tube, it's about enjoying a long stretch at the table with friends and family. The meal itself could be simple fare or the loftiest of haute cuisine. It doesn't matter. What matters is sharing a meal outside with people you care about. And the meal is the centerpiece of the evening and not simply a rush to the feedbag before getting back to gawking at screens of various sizes.

It's no wonder that the Italians came up with something called *The Slow Food Movement*. If left to us on this side of the pond, the movement would have been called *Reverse Liposuction*. So, let's take a cue from the Euros. It's time to enjoy a meal outside again with friends and family. What could be better? Otherwise, would you like another glass of Prosecco, Anita?

6-25-21

10

AIGS (EGGS)

"Oh, I frequently think every now

and then of the glorious fruit

of the noble hen

Eggs, eggs, E, double-G, S-eggs"

— DR. SEUSS

Eggs. Nature's perfect food in its most curious package. Since the dawn of time, mankind has been frying, poaching, boiling, deviling, scrambling, and sucking them in countless numbers. My own culinary egg history has a long cluck, beginning with visits to my maternal grandma's farm. There, she fried eggs up by the dozen in an ocean of reused bacon grease, serving them with steak and fried potatoes for my uncles. They would meet at her house early every morning for breakfast, except on weekends.

The three of them would show up separately in their Dodge pickups. Once inside, they'd take off their wide-brimmed cowboy hats and table any cigars already in progress. These were the cheap-ass cigars with green candela wrappers that smelled like burning dog turds. My grandpa had supposedly smoked them, so the boys did too.

Then, for the better part of an hour, my uncles would sit and drink huge cups of black coffee so strong it could have doubled as an industrial solvent. Grandma would fix them breakfast and fuss over them while wanting to know what was going on in every square inch of the farm.

My next egg memory is tied to an experiment during a Boy Scout outing. One spring weekend campout, my patrol decided to take one for the team and be the first to try out the dehydrated food that was being considered for the upcoming long-term summer camp. We consulted a list of victuals from a camping supply company that ranged from chipped beef—which sucks in any form—to a dessert called pineapple surprise. Of course, there were dried powdered eggs for rise and shine time.

I won't go into detail about how the weekend worked out. Let's just say that the members of my patrol spent a lot of time staring wistfully —and hungrily—at the fare being whipped up by the other patrols. Mornings were especially bad. Even when the directions were precisely followed, the eggs ended up looking and tasting like shredded Styrofoam packing material. I'm sure powdered eggs were developed by a plastics scientist. One look, one bite, and they probably thought, "we could sell this to U-Haul. And it will never degrade and collect in landfills for all time."

My next memory of eggs is from high school, getting ready for early morning fall marching band rehearsals. Martin, my dad, would insist on making me breakfast that consisted of a small glass of frozen OJ, two fried eggs, and a piece of almost-burnt toast with a small slab of near-frozen margarine that had somehow crash-landed on the black-ened surface. Martin had a way with eggs that consisted of a small frying pan, a bit of margarine or Crisco, and high heat. The recipe was simple. Fry the eggs until they stop talking. Flip them and repeat. If they don't bounce when they hit the plate, they're not done.

At some point during college, I moved from eggs over medium to ordering them sunny side up. For whatever reason, I liked the two yellow happy faces staring up at me from the plate. I also relished cutting around the yolks until it was time to pop them in my mouth and feel them go all runny and squishy. Carla remembers this strange culinary ritual from when we first started dating. It gave her the creeps. What was I thinking?

Here in New Mexico, eggs have always been the perfect vehicle for red or green chile—or both. The latter is called "Christmas" in the local vernacular. A personal favorite is huevos rancheros. I skip the beans now and just stick to the potatoes. Otherwise, the rancheros will stay with you long after the huevos have left the building.

Then there are deviled eggs. Of late, they've become a chichi and pricey appetizer in fine dining joints. Talk about gross margin. But they can be oh-so-good. Believe it or not, Champagne is a perfect match with spicy deviled eggs.

These days I stick to the tried-and-true soft scramble when it comes to personal egg styling. The soft scramble is not unlike doing the soft shoe. Both require the right timing and feel. The late Gregory Hines could do the soft shoe like no other. He probably ate his eggs soft scrambled as well. Too bad we couldn't have shared breakfast at some point. He could have shown me how to do the soft shoe. And I would have told him about Christmas.

6-14-21

11

A FEW OF MY FAVORITE FRIED THINGS

Frying food using various forms of fat, animal or otherwise, has long been a staple of mankind's diet. And who are we to question culinary history, even if it's a major cause of cardiovascular disease? But let's not dwell on that sordid aspect. Instead, we'll look on the bright side of life.

If one were to survey the general population on favorite foods, especially comfort foods, the frying-fat thing would be *the* common denominator. It's not like a poached salmon filet would top the list, much less even be mentioned. A salmon filet sauteed in butter with a squeeze of lemon might make a cameo, but only after all the other delicious comestibles were mentioned. With that, I'll take Julie Andrews' lead, at least from *The Sound of Music*, and list some of my favorite fried things. I'm also going to invite Julie to join me. I'm reasonably sure she'd agree to join the conversation. After all, the Brits are unusually adept at frying things. Wasn't it a Scottish chef who first figured out you could deep fry a Mars Bar with splendid results?

Before reading through my list, I'd pour Julie and me a glass of some-thing bubbly. Being a legendary actress/singer of stage and screen—and one of my big-time boyhood crushes—I'd opt for something rari-fied in the Champagne world like Bollinger RD or Pol Roger Cuvée Sir Winston Churchill. I'd also open a bag of chips because they happen to be near the top of the list. So, without further ado, here is a list of my favorite fried things with suggested beverage pairings included.

FRENCH FRIES

French fries might be the ultimate comfort food. Even when frozen and at their mediocre worst, French fries can be a thing of sizzling beauty. McDonald's, for one, has perfected the art of making tasty French fries on a mass, even global scale. They may be the only reason to ever darken a Mickie D's door. Otherwise, actual French fries, especially when cooked in goose fat or duck fat, are one of culinary life's greatest gifts. I'm reminded of one of the restaurants at the fabulous Montage Resort in Laguna Beach that once offered a French fry trio on their lunch menu. One of the options included tiny bits of shaved black truf-fles. What to drink with French fries? Non-vintage brut Champagne, with Gaston Chiquet and Delamotte among my favorites. By the way, the Brits call fries "chips." I'm sure Julie would approve of French fries, especially if paired with a tasty Champagne.

POTATO CHIPS

I have two questionable food habits, at least in the eyes of a cardiolo-gist. Well, maybe more than two. Regardless, one is chips. If I stop to think about it, the reason I finally threw in the towel and started to take a statin was because I was tired of feeling guilty every time I reached for a handful of chips. Mind you, the same goes for cheeseburgers and other things that will shortly make an appearance on this list. But chips are right up there in fried status with fries. And they don't have to be fancy. Lay's Classic will do nicely. But chips can also be a blank canvas on which to add any number of different flavorings: vinegar and salt, cheese of various kinds, and the ubiquitous BBQ. That aside, the Brits have perfected the art of crisps, as they call them.

Some years ago, I did a project with Frito-Lay International, developing varietal wine pairings with various flavors of their UK Walker's brand crisps. These weren't pedestrian flavors like those sold here in the U.S. Instead, they included more exotic offerings such as tandoori chicken and Thai-spice lime.

Otherwise, I don't want to neglect the corn chip universe. Fritos and Doritos are two personal favorites, especially the latter. I would go as far as to say that Nacho Cheese flavoring is one of mankind's greatest creations. As for beverages, if the chip bag was opened and passed around at cocktail hour, I'd still opt for bubbly of some kind. Champagne once again fits the bill, this time a non-vintage rosé brut from Billecart-Salmon or Laurent Perrier.

POPCORN

Though popcorn is not technically fried, making it requires some form of fat. One could do the microwave thing, though I find the faux-butter flavor a bit much. Inhaling diacetyl (butter flavor) has never been a favorite experience. That said, making popcorn using olive oil and then sprinkling it with sea salt, freshly cracked pepper, and a drizzle of melted butter is a recipe for temporary happiness. Bubbly things work best again, such as blanc de blancs Champagne like the non-vintage wines from Ruinart and Pierre Peters.

FISH AND CHIPS

And wrap them in newsprint, if you must. Paper aside, the mighty duo of breaded, fried cod filets and chips must surely have been handed down to Moses by God just after the ~~15~~ 10 commandments. When you're passing out the ultimate rules to life, you might as well include lunch. If done properly—meaning the oil is blazing hot—the combination of crispy crust and tender, flaky fish is a thing of perfection. And wait, fries are involved too. Does it get any better? As for beverages, something bubbly is once again needed. This time we'll opt for a selection from the beer universe. While one might be tempted to reach for a British ale like Samuel Smith or Newcastle, I recommend something a bit lighter like Pilsner Urquell or Bitburger. But in the end, the specific beer may mattereth not. It's the bubbles and tart acidity that do their magic dance on the palate, cleansing and preparing it for the next bite.

CHEESEBURGERS

As Samson is to Delilah, Romeo to Juliet, and Sodom to Gomorrah, so is the mighty cheeseburger to French fries—at least in terms of two things that go together. Thankfully, in this case, the pairing doesn't involve tragic haircuts, star-crossed lovers who do themselves in, or two cities bent on bad behavior and eternal damnation. Be all that as it may, cheeseburgers could be the ultimate comfort food. Frying a patty of fatty beef and serving it on a griddled hamburger bun with different condiments puts cheeseburgers at the top of the fried food pyramid, at the right hand of bacon. We'll get to the latter in just a moment.

What beverages go with cheeseburgers? The answer is many. Various soft drinks do the job, even diet cola with its after-taste reminiscent of PVC. Beer also comes to mind, and here one can go in any direction, including mass-produced commercial lagers like Coors or Budweiser, various IPA's like Lagunitas and DogFish Head, and the likes of Guinness Stout. If wine is desired, a big red like Biale Black Chicken Zinfandel or Langmeil Valley Floor Barossa Shiraz is perfect.

BACON

I've saved the best for last. First, the obvious: Bacon is the ne plus ultra of "vitamin P"–pork. If the FDA were ever to redo the food pyramid, bacon would rest atop with chocolate and Tater Tots just beneath. I'm sure Julie would agree that a rasher of bacon is the closest thing to

TIM GAISER, MS

fried culinary perfection that exists. What wines work with bacon? The answer is basically yes: rosé Champagne from Ruinart and Pol Roger, German Spätlese Riesling from Robert Weil or Gunderloch, or even uber-pricey Grand Cru red Burgundy like Robert Arnoux's Romanée Saint Vivant or Domaine Dujac's Clos de la Roche.

In the end, let us take a moment of silence and feel a bit of gratitude for the savory wonder of all things fried. After Julie and I sing "Climb Every Mountain," we'll close things out with a rousing rendition of "So Long, Farewell." And everything will be as it should.

3-27-23

12

BREAKING BREAD

There are many things I miss about San Francisco after living there for 33 years. The ocean, the bay, the hills, and Karl. Yes, I even miss Karl, the local name for the fog, especially during the blazing hot summer months now that I live in New Mexico. But there's something else uniquely San Franciscan that I miss dearly aside from the art museums, the symphony, and the amazing restaurant scene. What do I pine for? Bread. More specifically, sourdough bread as it can only be found in the City.

I love bread. Always have. When my siblings and I were kids, the six of us could easily hoover an entire loaf in one sitting, so mom bought bread in quantity and froze loaves in multiples. The brand of bread didn't matter. It was whatever was on sale along with the five-pound cans of MJB coffee in the big green can. Like any commercial ground coffee, MJB always smelled good when you first opened the can. Later, when I started drinking coffee and tried it, the stuff tasted like a cross between bile and battery acid. But my dad loved his pot of MJB in the morning. As much as the coffee, he loved his hour of peace and privacy with the morning paper before the rest of us got up and all hell broke loose, which happened on the regular.

A few times mom splurged and bought a loaf of Wonder Bread. I remember the white package with the festive red, yellow, and blue balloons, and the perfect slices with a spongy texture that reminded me of large flat marshmallows without the sugar. Even then I thought the stuff was like science gone wrong. But at least it provided more interest than the bland loaves of cheap white bread from the freezer that seemed to go instantly stale on the rare occasion they weren't inhaled on the spot.

I still eat impressive quantities of bread, usually with peanut butter. Some years ago, I went cold turkey on the huge jars of Jif I was buying at Costco after reading how much palm oil and salt they contain. Then the great peanut butter shortage of 2020 happened when the pandemic created a new syndrome called *blockheadia putzbrainia,* a condition that caused erstwhile intelligent adults to buy a lifetime supply of paper products in a single shopping trip leaving the rest of us in a wipe-twice lurch. The malady soon mapped over to other consumer goods including my beloved peanut butter. Mind you, it was a local phenomenon because a friend in Seattle had no problem masking up, going to her local market, and picking up a large jar of Skippy. She then generously sent it to me. Bless her for that.

After the peanut butter crisis passed, I eschewed big commercial brands and opted instead for *crunchy unsalted organic* from Sprouts (also a good personal description). It's pricier and needs refrigeration after opening. But now I'm only getting peanutty goodness and not chemicals, which is always a good thing as one ages.

Back to bread. Aside from sustenance, it's the ultimate food vehicle. With it, one can launch into an infinite number of possibilities, including spooning, spreading, and slathering condiments, comestibles, and sustainables. Sandwiches are a given. There's the classic Reuben with savory corned beef piled high accompanied by tart sauerkraut, Swiss cheese, and creamy dressing on earthy Jewish rye. Surely, the

Reuben occupies a spot in the top ten sandwich hall of fame. Curiously, the best Reuben I've ever had was not in New York, but at Charlie's Kosher Delicatessen in Los Angeles. It's also the largest sandwich I've ever consumed—and easily the most delicious.

There's also the classic BLT, where the bacon is always the star, with the tomato and lettuce in supporting roles. Hopefully, the tomato is ripe, and the lettuce is dry. As for the bread, it just needs to be good and doesn't have to change your life.

With the tried-and-true grilled cheese, the bread can also just be of good quality. But the cheese must be melty for the magic to happen. Velveeta would win the competition. But sometimes I think Velveeta is closer to industrial science more than anything.

I didn't experience bread as an art form until Carla and I went to Europe for the first time in 1987. There, the simplest ham and cheese on a baguette was a revelation. The croissants with our morning café au laits defied the laws of physics with a buttery density near that of dark matter. It was during the trip that I first realized that fresh bakery loaves are the coin of the bread realm.

For me, no artisan-baked loaf can top that of fresh sourdough, especially right out of the oven. There was a Boudin bakery store in the City in the Richmond District on 10th Ave., just up from Geary from where Carla used to work. Many times, I stopped there to pick up a sandwich on sourdough or a loaf baked earlier that morning on premise. It doesn't get better.

Here behind the adobe curtain, those who crave bakery bread usually flock to Whole Foods. Sadly, there is no store on this side of the river in Rio Rancho. Perhaps someday. In the meantime, the pursuit of good bread has us driving 25 minutes to one of two Whole Foods stores in Burque Flats (Albuquerque). My son Patrick and I did that last week, hoping to pick up a loaf of sourdough. We opted for a loaf of rosemary sourdough, even better. And we didn't pass up on the large brown butter chocolate chip cookies. Why would you?

Over the years, Carla has told me that when she was growing up one of the catch phrases when her family was starting a meal was being offered toast or Kleenex. The idea must have been that either or both would have made the meal complete. I couldn't agree more.

Rumor has it that additives are now being used in commercially produced bread that make a loaf smell fresh long after opening. Those same additives keep the bread soft and pliable even in Sahara-like conditions like here in the high desert. I wonder how long it will be before the same additives find their way into supplements for geriatrics. Regardless, I think the freshener-softener thing is completely unnecessary. One can always make toast. Or if feeling a bit fancy, one can always cube the bread and make croutons. Et voila!

These days the media is filled with warnings about AI and how it will take over our lives in the years to come. How there may come a time in the future when humans are no more necessary than the pre-packaged condiments you get at Wendy's. Hopefully, I won't be around then. But I have a feeling that bread will be. Even sourdough. And peanut butter, too which means there will be toasters. And spring rain. I think Ray Bradbury said that. He was right.

12-20-22

13

YOU CALL THAT CHEESE?

During my last shopping trip to Whole Foods, one of the drive-by, toss-in-the-cart-without-stopping purchases was a package of sliced cheese labeled "Swiss." By the way, this is the same technique I use for buying Pringles at Target. The technique where you don't stop the cart and nab the Pringles as you go by. Otherwise, I've settled into using cheese slices for sandwiches. It's among the many food concessions made since moving back behind the adobe curtain. Likewise, so is eating more frozen food than ever before.

As for the package of cheese slices, on closer examination the fine print on the front said, "imported from Switzerland." So at least it had truth in origin going for it. The cheese itself was decent in that it tasted similar to other actual Swiss cheeses of quality like Emmentaler, which cheese experts describe as "nutty." To me, it just tasted like cheese. Or grown-up cheese, I should say. That's because Swiss cheese with any flavor to it is an acquired taste, at least for kids. Tasting it for the first time--even the mass-produced stuff--may seem like alien nation. It's as remote from the bricks of yellow-orange Longhorn Cheddar as possible.

Unless you grow up in a household that makes exotic foodstuffs the norm, you probably won't embrace anything cheese-wise other than Kraft singles and the previously mentioned Longhorn until early adulthood. Around that same time, Dijon mustard (not actually from Dijon), garlic, and espresso may also cross your radar—all delightful and very grown-up things.

Back to cheese and a recent Rhône River cruise. Specifically, the day we were docked in Lyon. It was a Monday and happened to be a holiday, *la fête de la Victoire* or *le jour de la libération.* Literally, WWII Victory Day, the anniversary of when Charles de Gaulle announced the end of World War II in France on May 8, 1945. No surprise that traffic was a fraction of what it usually was. The first stop that morning for my compadres, Paul and Margaret, and me was the Paul Bocuse Market. Chef Bocuse has long been a legend in Lyon and environs. Although Paris gets all the glam and cred, Lyon is known even in France as the food center of the country. And restaurant Paul Bocuse has crested atop three-star Michelin establishments for decades, even after the great chef passed away in 2018.

Over 80% of the vendors at the Paul Bocuse Market had taken the day off, it being a holiday. The few vendors who chose to open were more than worth the price of admission—which was free. Missing were the florists and produce vendors, but present were several butchers and fromageries. Per the latter, cheese is important in France. Every region, however small or large, has its own cheese(s) made from the milk of local cows, sheep, or goats. More than a few have taken their place in the global cheese pantheon. Brie, Camembert, Roquefort, and Chèvre, just to name a few. There are easily hundreds more, as witnessed by the sheer number of cheeses on display at several fromageries at the market that day. One vendor in particular easily had over 120 cheeses immaculately displayed, a fraction of which can be seen in the photo below.

Paul, Margaret, and I stopped and admired the sumptuous display. Then Margaret chatted at length in French with the young woman who was the fromagère. Her first question was when we would be enjoying the cheeses. As it turns out, timing in the cheese world—as with many other things—is important. Margaret informed mademoiselle fromagère that we would be enjoying one of the cheeses that evening with another the following day and a third cheese the day after. With that information, a selection of cheeses was made and then immaculately wrapped in special paper and tied up decoratively with bits of ribbon. Finally, everything was carefully placed in a small attractive tote bag.

After a walk through the botanical gardens, we made our way back towards the river and our lunch destination, a bistro called Daniel & Denise. We arrived shortly before noon and were seated at a table with large pieces of white butcher paper atop a red and white checkered tablecloth. In no time we were greeted by our waiter, an affable young man. Between Margaret's French and his fractured English, the twain did meet. Paul ordered braised beef ribs, Margaret opted for sauteed calf's liver, and I had chicken tournedos with morel sauce. We went local in our wine selection: a bottle of cru Beaujolais, a Fleurie under the restaurant's label. It was delicious and perfect with the meal.

After a bit of a wait, the entrees appeared. As affable young waiter guy placed my plate in front of me, I got a waft of intense mushroom, cream, and chicken. It was precisely at this moment when I was glad for once I was on a statin. God knows how much butter and cream were involved just in the sauce. It probably bordered on dark matter. Then the sides came. A dynamic duo of the best mac and cheese I've ever had with incredible potatoes, roasted in goose fat. There must have been at least three different cheeses in the mac and cheese, all in the triple cream realm. Not only was it rich beyond imagination, but the flavor was amazing, reminding me of mademoiselle fromagère and her impressive selection of cheeses in the market earlier that morning.

Later, after getting back to the ship, I ran into Margaret who was leaving her cabin with the cheese tote bag in tow. "They're too strong to keep in the room," she said, shaking her head. I nodded and immediately glanced off a force field of raw cheeseness redolent of a locker room crossed with a dairy. Margaret took the cheeses to the kitchen for proper storage with a request for one of them to be served to us that night at the end of dinner.

That evening's cheese turned out to be a Chèvre made from raw goat's milk. After the entrées were cleared, our server brought us the small wheel of Chèvre with some sliced baguette. It was easily the best goat cheese I've ever had. It was also the most feral goat cheese I've ever tasted with a pungent rind and creamy interior that was a solid "10" on the goat scale. I'd never had a goat cheese like it. And unless I'm in France, I probably never will again.

Raw milk cheeses are an exotic creature in the U.S. because the dairy and cheese industries are heavily regulated. The most contentious law is the FDA-mandated pasteurization of all milk products for consumption that was passed in 1987. Per the law, all milk must be heated to 145°F (63°C) for at least 30 minutes or at least 161°F (72°C) for 15 seconds. The idea being to rid the milk of pathogenic bacteria, making it safe to consume, and to kill enzymes that cause spoiling so as to give the product a longer shelf life.

At the time—almost 40 years ago—the judge in the case ruled that unpasteurized milk was unsafe and banned the shipment of any raw milk with the exception of cheese, provided it had been aged a minimum of 60 days and clearly labeled as unpasteurized. However, there was a catch. Many of the most famous raw milk cheeses like Camembert, Roquefort, and Brie won't stay fresh on the shelf for more than 10 days, meaning they couldn't survive the legally required period of aging. To add insult to injury, in 2014 the FDA lowered the limit of nontoxigenic E. coli, a harmless form of the bacteria found in our digestive tract, from 100 MPN (most probable number) to 10 MPN, meaning that even small levels can prevent cheeses from being imported into the U.S.

The intent behind the pasteurization law was to prevent people from being poisoned by bacteria-tainted milk and cheese. However, it should also be noted that less than 2,000 cases of illness from consuming raw milk and dairy products were reported in the U.S. between 1993 and 2012.

As for the other two cheeses from the Bocuse Market, we enjoyed one with lunch the next day and the last with the penultimate dinner the night after. Both were rich, creamy, decadent, and frankly on the ripe side. Like attractive but unwashed people. Beyond the unkempt part, the two were also completely delicious and unlike any domestic cheeses I've ever tasted.

Afterwards, I wondered if all real cheeses, as in those made from raw milk, tasted this way. As in rich and creamy but slightly funky and smelly. In which case, have all my cheese experiences in the US been neutered because of the laws? I think you know the answer. I then wondered if tasting this kind of cheese would always be a uniquely French experience, or at the very least European. That is, until the Byzantine FDA laws change. I decided not to hold my breath on that one.

Thankfully, there's no shortage of outstanding domestic cheeses to choose from, including raw milk cheeses. But the latter must be aged 60 days as per the law. In the end, context in cheese matters as with everything else in life. Which means I'll probably still swipe right for Swiss singles the next time I'm at Whole Foods. But I'll make sure not to stop the cart. After all, rules are rules.

6-1-23

14

2 + 2 = TACOS

Taking a cue from good friend and fellow MS, Evan Goldstein, I tend to put food and wine pairings into three distinct categories. First, there's "Switzerland," where the dish and the wine stay in their own lanes and refuse to interact, not unlike a group of middle school kids at a dance. The opposite is "train wreck in the mouth," where the food and wine clash so epically, so ecumenically, and so severely, that even the thought of the combination can immediately cause human pathos and suffering. A good example would be oysters on the half shell with a tannic Cabernet Sauvignon. No further explanation needed.

Finally, there are magic combinations in which a pairing transcends the individual food and wine components involved. Evan calls these pairings "2 + 2 = 5." A good example would be a botrytis dessert wine such as Sauternes paired with a salty blue cheese like Stilton. To this category I would also add pairing Champagne with popcorn or potato chips. All the tiny bubbles are a perfect dancing partner with the carbohydrates, salt, and just the right touch of fat. Speaking of fat, I would be remiss if I didn't mention bacon. It's a category—a culinary universe—all to its own. I think you can drink practically any decent wine, regardless of style, with good bacon.

Then there's tacos. Having just now looked online, I can pass on a bit about the history of the humble and yet noble taco. The name comes from the Nahuatl word "tlahco" which means "half or in the middle," referring to the way a taco is formed. Back in the day, soft corn tortillas filled with fish and cooked organ meat were a staple.

The modern taco, if we can call it that, was introduced to the U.S. in the early 20th century when Mexican migrants came to this country to work on the railroads and in mines. However, many gringos were first exposed to the mighty taco through Mexican food carts in Los Angeles and other SoCal environs run by women called "chili queens." By then, organ meat and other traditional exotic fillings had been replaced by ground beef and chicken, not to mention the now ubiquitous lettuce, tomato, and onions.

The rest, as they say, is cultural culinary history, with food trucks still being the urtext of taco-dom by offering the purest expression of folded tortilla art. But the taco universe is vast. If one feels the urge, there's always a quick drive-through/drive-by south of the border experience at Taco Bell. If anything, the latter proves the invincibility of the taco. I would go as far as to say that the taco is the baseball of popular food culture in that it can't be broken. With baseball, regardless of all the changes to the game over the years (including the infield fly rule, the designated hitter, and the recently adopted pitch clock), the game is still its brilliant and pure self.

Tacos, too, remain clearly identifiable despite various attempts to make them into gaudy culinary gewgaws. It's not unreasonable then to assume that tacos could easily fall into Evan's last category with the combination of savory, salty, and fatty elements being a veritable launching pad for practically any style of wine including personal favorites like Bohemia and Modelo Especial. Otherwise, I'll cast my vote for tacos being the ultimate comfort food. Because there are times when we all just want tacos.

6-28-22

15

ROMAINES OF THE DAY

The idea of eating mixed greens with some kind of dressing goes back to the ancient Greeks and Romans. But the word salad entered the English language from the French *salade,* itself a shortened form of the Latin *herba salata* (salted herb), also from the Latin *salata,* ultimately from *sal* (salt). The word first appears in English in the 14th century as *sallet.* All the variations have to do with salt because going back to Roman times, vegetables were seasoned with brine, salty oil, or vinegar. Shakespeare first used the phrase "salad days" in 1606 to mean a time of youthful inexperience. Closer to home, or your nearest Cracker Barrel, the first salad bar was offered in 1937. By the 50s, these salad buffets were common fixtures in restaurants like mutant offspring of the Scandinavian smorgasbord, but sans Aquavit.

Childhood salad memories involve large plastic bowls filled with lettuce, which was usually chopped iceberg. From there, any number of veggies were added, including chunky slices of under ripe tomatoes, sliced cucumbers, and chopped green bell peppers. Sometimes grated longhorn cheese was sprinkled over the top to make the entire affair more continental. Ingredients aside, any salad even then was all about the dressing, and any dressing in the time of my youth came in a store-bought bottle. French Dressing, with its dull orange sheen, was all the rage. Only years later did I learn it was basically mayo with a splash of ketchup for color. As time went on, Zesty Italian, Ranch, and Thousand Island were added to the dressing stable. My favorite then, beyond the tried-and-true French, was Kraft's Zesty Italian made from the foil packet. If you mixed it with sour cream, it also made a savory dip for chips. Can you say versatile?

I also remember my Grandma Wade's Jell-O salads, and not because I liked them. As a little kid, I found the texture of Jell-O unnerving. The way it wiggled long after impact was unsightly at best. That it could be found in any color of the rainbow except blue only empha-sized the fact that you were eating something made by the chemical industrial complex. And once my older siblings Tina and Tom let me in on the not-so-well-kept secret that Jell-O was made from gelatin, which was made from the skins and hooves of dead animals, the deal was sealed. I passed on anything resembling Jell-O forever more. That especially went for granny's Jell-O salads that compounded the gelatin fracture with added slices of Dole pineapple and cottage cheese. Think about it. A ring-shaped green Jell-O salad made milky and murky with streaks of cottage cheese curds and chunks of canned pineapple slices. The only thing missing were Vienna sausages.

A major shift in the salad universe occurred once we moved to Ann Arbor so I could attend grad school. Then the combination of my wife Carla working at the Earle restaurant and us dining periodically at my trumpet professor, Armando Ghitalla's home brought the realization that salad did not have to be served until after the entrée. Historically, it was intended to cleanse the palate after the heaviness of the main course, which was usually some form of protein. The Earle also dialed up more exotic fare in the greens universe, including the Salade Niçoise and the classic Caesar. The former was a revelation in that a salad with the right protein and veggies could be a complete meal.

With the Caesar, the idea that salad dressing could register on the culinary Richter scale with serious quantities of garlic and anchovies.

From then on, salad in the Peña-Gaiser household would be forever more served after the entrée and before any cheese or sweets. But I wonder if it was Escoffier who first moved the salad to post-entrée. Or was it an aspect of formal Russian service, at least the part where you weren't invading each other's stations? Regardless, around the same time, Carla honed her chops to the all-pro level when it came to making salad dressings from scratch. Her specialty is Caesar dressing. Even though the ingredients have always remained the same, each batch is slightly different. But the common denominators of bracing acidity, pungent garlic, and anchovy bite are always there.

There are times when I think one can measure the quality of a restaurant not by how clean it keeps its restrooms—although true—but how well the kitchen dresses a salad. More often than not, a restaurant salad is a mass of prepackaged greens glopped to the gills with a dressing with the texture of sludge. The longer the twain do meet, the more one understands how peat bogs are formed. However, there are times when one is served a salad comprising absolutely fresh greens that are carefully washed, thoroughly dried, and hand-dressed with just the right touch of house-made vinaigrette. It's a thing of vegetative beauty.

Here at the compound, salads are practically always part of the dinner menu. Usually, the greens are dished out of a plastic container, what with our living behind the adobe curtain. But the quality is variable. Purchase any salad offering from a mass brand supermarket, even those labeled "organic," and you're forking over shekels for what could double as lawn clippings. It's like the greens were rinsed in a car wash and then put through a wind tunnel for the dry cycle. Good salad greens, on the other hand, come from Sprouts or Whole Foods. With either, you're getting high quality stuff that's not only fresh but washed multiple times, so good to go upon opening. As for dressings, we run the gambit from Carla's specialties to store-bought bottles of Girard's, once a Bay Area delicacy and now made in an elephant graveyard of condiments.

In the end, my favorite salad is still the Caesar. I've even included it as one of the courses in my "meal for the end of time" (see Chapter 45). An imaginary literal last supper when the world is about to end in biblical fashion with mountains crumbling, rivers of fire, and cats and dogs living together in sin. As for the salad, the romaine has to be utterly crisp, the croutons crunchy and freshly baked, and the dressing pungent with garlic and bracingly acidic. One last thing. Don't skimp on the anchovies, please.

7-23-23

PART THREE

WINE

No surprise that some of the longest and weightiest chapters in the book are about wine. In particular, the book's title chapter, "Strong Water," is a personal manifesto on all things vinous. However, lest you be tempted to flee to the section on humor, rest assured that all the entries in this section of the book are straightforward, easy to follow, and lack any *you kids get off my lawn* sentiment. Otherwise, many of the following chapters are quasi-instructional in that I explain terms for wine texture, discuss how climate change is altering the landscape of wine education, and offer how my training and career in classical music helped me pass the Master Sommelier exams. There's also a cautionary tale about the perils of carelessly opening a bottle of sparkling wine. Be forewarned. And read on.

16

WINE EPIPHANY NO. 2

It was the spring of 1989, a momentous time. Carla was pregnant with our daughter Maria, who would be born at the end of August. For the next few months, we lived in a stylish sixth floor apartment on Russian Hill in the City, with spectacular views of the Bay and Alcatraz. But impending parenthood would soon have us relocate to a place in Pacific Heights. It may have been just 16 blocks away, but the new apartment was in a completely different universe.

At the time, I was bartending at Bix Restaurant in the Jackson Square District. Within months of taking the job, I was also helping with the wine buying. Part of that equation was to attend trade tastings and events. The most memorable of these industry gatherings—even now over thirty years later—was a seminar put on by Remy Martin, the venerable Cognac house.

The session was billed as a Cognac master class and blending seminar. The venue for the event was a ballroom in the posh Ritz Carlton Hotel above Union Square. There was no parking anywhere near the hotel. My options for two hours of temporary vehicle lodging were to either use the Ritz Valet or park at the Sutter-Stockton Garage and walk several blocks up a very steep hill. I did the latter only to arrive fairly sweaty just before the seminar started.

The presentation began with a welcome from an executive VP from the importer. After some initial chit chat, the presenter was introduced. He was Remy's Chef de Cave, the supremely olfactory-gifted individual whose job it was to finalize all the blends for the house's Cognacs; from the humble V.S. to the sublime and sublimely expensive Louis XIII, which even at the time retailed for over a thousand dollars a bottle.

The Chef de Cave, or CdC as I'll call him, started the proceedings by talking about the history of Remy Martin vis-à-vis the rest of the region and industry. How Remy, of the four major houses, was the smallest and had access to more grapes from vineyards in the top subzones, those being Grande Champagne and Petite Champagne. Access to more high-quality vineyards resulted in better overall quality in the Remy Cognacs vs. the competition. It should be noted that the term "Champagne" in the context of Cognac has nothing to do with the named place or its sparkling wines. Instead, the name is derived from the Latin *campagna*, which translates as field.

Next, we tasted through several single component brandies made from the six subzones, including the two previously mentioned. Then we made our own blend, using information on the styles of all the single subzone brandies just given. Finally, we tasted through the entire line of Remy Martin Cognacs, ending with the aforementioned Louis XIII. I found the *Louis Tres*, as it is called, to be light and ethereal on the palate but also to have remarkable concentration and length. It's one of the greatest spirits I've ever tasted.

At some point during the last round of tasting, the CdC offered a primer on smelling Cognac. Taking a small tulip glass in hand, he told the group that to properly smell Cognac—or any distilled spirit for that matter—there were as many as five different positions used to examine the contents of the glass. The first position was holding the glass 12-15 inches away from one's nose. Then one moved the glass closer slowly in increments of several inches. The penultimate smelling position was with the glass about two inches away from one's nose. The final position was to smell the brandy with one's nose in the glass.

Then the CdC took the group through the technique using one of the brandies. The result was immediately evident. Even with the glass far away, I could still smell delicate floral and fruit qualities in the brandy. Each successive smelling position brought new aromatics to the fore, with hints of various fruits, spices, earth, and the oak used in the aging process.

As good as this new technique was, the CdC wasn't finished. "You know," he said, "for some of you the alcohol in these brandies may be too strong for your nose. You need to pull the glass away from your face a little bit. Then open your mouth slightly and smell by breathing through your mouth and nose at the same time."

Being Cognac devotees and eager acolytes, we immediately followed his advice. The reaction from the group was mixed. For many, the change made no noticeable difference. A few found smelling through the mouth and nose at the same time impossible. It was like they'd been asked to throw a baseball with their off hand. Then there were the outliers like me.

I quickly picked up a glass, brought it to within an inch of my nose, and then opened my mouth about a quarter of an inch. At first, smelling using both my nose and mouth seemed alien. But within a few seconds, everything changed. I could smell more than twice as much as before, and all the aromatics in the glass jumped out faster than I could recognize them.

After a few seconds, I put the glass down and stared ahead, stunned. Up to that point, I had struggled with smelling wines and spirits. There were times when it seemed like I was missing half of what everyone else was getting. But now in an instant everything had changed. Somehow, the simple act of pulling the glass away and using mouth and nose to smell changed everything. It was like the bright lights, chorus of singing angels, and enchilada plate Christmas all rolled into one.

From there, I quickly went back and tried the technique combined with the five different positions. Even with the glass far away, I could now smell considerably more by just opening my mouth slightly. It was like turning up the volume on a quality sound system so everything could be easily heard. And the closer I brought the glass to my face, the more detailed the Cognac in hand became.

After the fact, I came to call this nose/mouth combination *active inhalation* vs. the *passive inhalation* of just smelling using one's nose. This combination actually makes physiological sense given there are two ways to smell. The first is using the nose only and is called orthonasal smell. The other uses the oral cavity and sinuses and is called retronasal smell. Retronasal smell uses a much larger internal area to process aromas.

Most of the human race uses orthonasal to smell wine, in that they stick their nose in a wine glass and go for it. Conversely, a few people like me use both ortho and retronasal smelling in sequence when we smell.

I quickly discovered something else about the new smelling technique. By pulling the glass away at varying distances, I could improve my sensitivity to the aromas in a wine to the extent of being able to detect trace amounts.

I've taught the *active inhalation* technique to thousands of students over the years. The results are usually mixed like they were during that first seminar. There's no change for most people who try active inhalation for the first time. A few students can't do it at all. But for some, it's revelatory. One time a student came up to me after a class saying he had issues with a cleft palate, and that by smelling through nose and mouth he could actually detect something in a glass of wine for the first time.

I sometimes think back to the seminar at the Ritz long ago and how the Chef de Cave gave me one of the most valuable lessons I have ever learned about smelling spirits—and wine. I only wish I could have gotten his name so I could have thanked him. In lieu of that, I'll just say *mille merci, mon ami.*

4-18-22

17

WINE TEXTURE TERMS
DEFINED

Some years ago, I was in Hong Kong for a set of MS classes and exams. It was my first time there. The day before class started, our local contact took us to one of his favorite haunts for lunch. It was a hole-in-the-wall joint that specialized in noodles. The owner called out as we entered and beckoned us to take a seat at a small table in the corner. The chairs were plastic and on their last legs. Literally. The table wobbled like a wounded steer and was covered with a dingy plastic tablecloth that may have been white at one time, but now had a mottled texture not unlike the photos you see of the surface of Mars.

A rapid-fire exchange in Mandarin followed, with our colleague ordering a sampling of what the kitchen had to offer. One of the first dishes to hit the table was a bowl filled with a shiny gelatinous substance that jiggled. "Jellyfish," our colleague said, "it's a delicacy." In true *when in Rome fashion,* we helped ourselves to a serving of the steaming, ever-moving mass and tucked in. The smell and flavor were vaguely ocean-like, but the texture dominated the experience. I can only describe it as a combination of slimy and gooey combined with the al dente of pasta fame. The slimy part of the equation reminded me of boiled okra from my childhood and my maternal grandma's dinner table. That memory quickly morphed into various iterations of snot.

My janky reverie was interrupted when the second dish appeared. It featured noodles in chicken broth with small grayish cubes of what appeared to be tofu. "Cured pig's blood," our colleague said. "It's good for you. Cleans the system." Assuming the stance of an adventurous diner once again, I helped myself to a small portion making sure the noodles outweighed the cured pig blood bits by a factor of ten-to-one. Then, for the sake of science, I took a bite. What followed was a mix of familiar and alien, as in noodles and broth with strong livery overtones. The texture of the bits could only be described as squishy. The liver part also brought back childhood memories, but more along tragic lines concerning my dad's love of calf liver, my mom's inability to cook it, and us kids being made to eat it. There was even a time when I had cold liver for lunch only because I wouldn't eat it for breakfast. And that was because I refused to eat it for dinner the night before. I will say no more.

Our lunch that day was far from the only culinary standout during the trip. Practically every meal offered something new and different, if not strange. A special merit award went to sea cucumber, which we had several times. It combined the gooey-slimy duo with crunchy and bitter, all the while featuring a strong marine-life aftertaste. It paired best with the favorite local wine called Tsingtao.

Recently, I thought of the Hong Kong trip with all its culinary delicacies after reading an article in the Times called "Why Do American Diners Have Such a Limited Palate for Textures?" It was written by Ligaya Mishan. The upstart of the article was this: Compared to other cultures, especially those in Asia, the U.S. has a limited range of favorite food textures and words to describe them. Mishan begins the article with an ode to jellyfish:

"A jellyfish tastes of nothing. Maybe a little salt — a trace of the sea, or of how the creature is packed, once wrested from its natural habitat, for preservation (not of its life but of its viability as food). When its bell is prepared as a raw salad, it tastes only of the ingredients it absorbs: a sluice of soy sauce, sesame oil and black vinegar, scattered garlic, a pinch of sugar. What makes it coveted as a dish in some cultures is the texture, which is nothing like jelly at all. The flesh wobbles but doesn't deliquesce; instead, it resists, crunching under the teeth, because a jellyfish is almost half made of collagen, the connective tissue whose braided strands run through skin and bone."

You get the picture. There are places in the world inhabited by hundreds of millions of people where slimy as a food texture is not only tolerated, but a favorite. Mishan writes that a 2008 article in the *Journal of Texture Studies* (yes, there is such a thing) lists 144 terms used by the Chinese for food texture, including various grades of what we would call crunchy. For example, there's *cui nen* for tender but crisp (bamboo shoots and spring Asparagus), *su song* for crisp and loose (simmered pork shredded and dried), and *su ran* which translates as brittle then soft like pastry so flaky it dissolves when touched.

Japanese textural terms outdo the Chinese by a factor of three, with the report listing over 400. Mishan highlights several Japanese terms for what we call crunchy including *shaki shaki* for a gushy bite (apple right off the tree), *saku saku* for pork skins dropped in hot oil where they expand like clouds, *gari gari* for a hard crunch like chewing ice cubes, *bari bari* for the delicate crunching of a rice cracker, and *pari pari* for the "evanescent shattering" of potato chips. Yes, all those just to describe crunchy things. There's no mention of what the Italians called al dente in pasta or what the Taiwanese call "Q" or "QQ" in noodles and boba. For the record, my favorite Japanese food term is *neba neba*, for things that are slimy or gooey.

Mishan then asks why the American palate is so limited when it comes to preferred textures in food as well as words used to describe them. She offers several theories, first noting that there have always been differences in what people eat based on the flora and fauna available to them--which is based on climate and geography. She also points to Europe being less biodiverse than Asia, Africa, and South America, making for a narrower range of available foodstuffs. Mishan then writes about the development of a so-called "food hierarchy" centuries ago with a much broader range of flavors and textures. Then the nobility and well-to-do had a wealth of foodstuffs to choose from while the average Joe couldn't afford to be picky. For the masses, nothing was wasted and every possible bit of an animal was consumed. It goes without saying that offal was considered anything but awful.

WINE TEXTURES

Unlike food, descriptors for wine texture number far more than the garden variety "smooth" and "crunchy." Practically all the descriptors are based on a wine's structural elements, those being the levels of residual sugar, acidity, alcohol, phenolic bitterness, and tannin—and combinations thereof. Texture in wine is also more subjective and based on an individual's tolerance of, or preference for, these structural elements. For example, one person may be averse to anything with high acidity in food and drink while another craves it. The same goes for tannin and residual sugar.

The point is that we may all have the same brain and nervous system but we each come with a unique set of sensory programming. With that, here's a list of commonly used texture terms for wine plus a few additions to the menu that attempt to describe a wine's character— which again is based on texture due to structural elements. In a few cases, there are terms that have always puzzled me. I note them as appropriate. Keep in mind these are my definitions and nothing is written in stone. After all, you may call smooth red wines Hello Kitty and tannic red wines Mothra. It's your prerogative.

A LIST OF WINE TEXTURE TERMS

Angular: a term sometimes used to describe a young wine with high acid, moderate alcohol, and not quite enough fruit to back it all up. The term disjointed is similarly used. Both terms may also imply that a wine is straightforward but will hopefully develop as time goes on.

Astringent: implies harsh tannin on the finish of a red wine due to either youth, too much oak, or the wine having been made from a tannic grape like Nebbiolo (Barolo and Barbaresco). Remember, not every red wine can be like Hello Kitty.

Austere: what I've always taken from this descriptor is that the wine in question is not fun to drink. Regardless, I would assume that the wine is bone-dry with high acidity, less alcohol, and not a lot of fruit. It's like a sweet tart without the sweet part.

Bright: seems to imply a young wine with lots of youthful aromatics, vibrant (tart) fruit, and high acidity.

Chewy: tannin here again the culprit. A chewy red wine brings to mind the fact that tannin is used to cure leather. A moment of pause while we consider what it likewise probably does to our palates.

Creamy: a white wine term that signifies lees contact was used in the aging process. The creamy descriptor might also point to the use of malolactic fermentation resulting in the buttery aroma and flavor from the chemical diacetyl.

Crisp: a wine with elevated acidity. The descriptor "tart" is also used.

Dense: I have to add the term "dry extract" here. In chemist parlance, it means solids in solution. In wine, it means grape solids in solution after fermentation and any fining and filtration. Dry extract is measured in grams per liter, and a wine with high dry extract is usually made from a vineyard with older vines and lower yields. A wine with high dry extract is also richer and more full-bodied, regardless of the alcohol level. That said, red wines are sometimes described as dense when they have concentrated fruit, which could also be the result of high dry extract.

Elegant: often used to describe wines like Pinot Noir that have moderate tannins and a good fruit/acid balance. In other words, a lighter red wine that is smooth. We'll get to smooth in a moment.

Fat: the first stage in describing a wine with an abundance of ripe (or overripe) fruit, elevated alcohol, and barely enough acidity to balance it.

Flabby: the second stage of the previous term with a distinct lack of acidity. Inexpensive, commercial Gewürztraminer comes to mind.

Fleshy: this one has always puzzled me. Fleshy like what? Animal flesh? (see cured pig's blood above). I may be wrong here, but I take it to mean a red wine with concentrated fruit and softer tannins.

Gritty: astringent, as in a young Cabernet Sauvignon with lots of unresolved tannin. Hence the need for aging. Or if the wine is served when young, decant it and pair it with a source of protein with salt and fat. It's why Cabernet pairs so well with a grilled ribeye steak.

Heavy: a wine described as heavy usually denotes ripe/overripe fruit, high alcohol, and modest acidity. "Clunky" is another destination on the vinous road to heaviness. Ditto "ponderous."

Jammy: often used to describe Zinfandel with ripe, overripe, and even raisinated fruit. High alcohol and added acidity are usually part of the package.

Juicy: describes what I call the sweet-tart factor, which is a balance of fruit and acidity. A juicy wine implies one with plenty of youthful fruit balanced by elevated acidity. Think young Chenin Blanc or blush wines.

Lean: A lean wine is one with high acidity, moderate alcohol, and in need of more fruit. Lean wines are also sometimes mineral-driven. While they may not be the best choice to sip from a plastic cup next to the pool, they can be versatile food wines.

Linear: another term that's perennially puzzled me. Does linear mean straightforward, as in simple? If anything, linear might be a running mate with lean. Both denote less fruit and higher acidity.

Oily: a term I've heard used to describe the texture of Alsace Gewürztraminer, a rich, concentrated white wine without a lot of acidity. I've also heard oily used to describe the texture of Alsace Pinot Gris.

Opulent: opulent is rich taken to the next degree. Both terms imply a white or red with an abundance of ripe fruit with just enough acidity to balance. The red would also have soft tannins.

Rich: the above to a lesser degree. The recipe calls for ripe, concentrated fruit, higher alcohol, and less natural acidity--which means the wine may be acidulated.

Sharp: makes me think of red wines made from grapes like Sangiovese that are very dry with high acidity and more than their fair share of tannin.

Silky: a red wine with soft tannins made from a grape like Pinot Noir. It's not like you're going to describe Petite Sirah as silky. More like monster truck pull. Elegant is often used in conjunction with silky.

Smooth: the most widely used descriptor for the favorite style of red wine by American consumers, surely an extension of the Starbucks Frappuccino gestalt. Just kidding. Smooth red wines are those without a lot of tannin.

Soft: a variation of the smooth theme, meaning less tannin and more fruit in a red wine, and without high acidity. White wines can also be soft, in which case there's ample fruit but also a lack of acidity.

Steely: I've always taken this to mean a white wine like Chablis with pronounced minerality and high acidity.

Structured: a puzzler. All wines have structure, don't they? Perhaps describing a wine as structured means that it's balanced but probably on the younger, undeveloped side. In which case, the acid/tannin combo may need some time to come together.

Succulent: the sweet-tart thing again but this time with some residual sugar. I think of Vouvray Demi-Sec and German Auslese Riesling as succulent. The best examples of both have the capacity to be other-worldly and temporarily change your life.

Supple: used with red wines with lots of fruit and soft tannins. Supple is often used to describe Merlot.

Tight: a descriptor for a young red wine with elevated acidity and firm tannins. Also, a wine that needs decanting and air time before drinking (or a few years in the cellar).

Velvety: a member of the silky/smooth club and a common descriptor for Pinot Noir.

Voluptuous: used to describe a white or red wine with an overabundance of ripe fruit and just barely enough acidity to support it.

Viscous: to me, viscous means a wine with high dry extract. In other words, regardless of the alcohol level, there's a lot of "there" there, making for a richer wine.

Waxy: as described. Wines made from the Sémillon grape are often described as having a waxy texture or sensation on the palate.

5-13-23

18

THE ICE FLOW IS DRIFTING

One of the more important features in my tasting book, *Message in the Bottle: A Guide to Tasting Wine*, is the lists of grape variety descriptions ranging from the tried-and-true Cabernet Sauvignon, Merlot, and Chardonnay to more obscure and esoteric entries like Melon de Bourgogne, Carignan, and Pinotage.

While many in the industry and consumers alike probably welcomed these detailed descriptions, I'm waiting for the inevitable naysayers to appear. When they do, they'll vociferously complain about the exact way I describe the grapes and wines, their argument being that this kind of specificity and precision is an illusion and doesn't exist. That the grapes and wines I list in the book have changed, are changing at the moment, and will continue to change in the future due to global warming.

To which I respond, all true. There are precious few things about wine that are precise.

But wines described as "classic" have been made from specific grapes grown in certain places for a long time. Hence the term itself, which implies a lengthy track record of quality. What these classic wines also tend to display is a commonality of style marked by vintage variation, also the result of climate change.

Learning classic wines has been one of the mainstays of formal industry education for as long as it's existed. Historically, students pursuing various wine certifications have had to study reams of geography about major growing regions around the globe and then learn the respective grape varieties and wines.

I've taught tasting at every level for over three decades. Two key elements of wine education are learning dozens of terms used to describe what's in the glass, and consistent practice using a tasting grid of some kind. The sum total can be daunting for students. Chunking down the information into manageable bits is important for the instructor. And being able to explain things so a kid can understand them, as the great physicist Richard Feynman supposedly once said, is key. Otherwise, the amount of information can be overwhelming.

Learning markers for dozens of classic grapes and wines has long been a part of any wine curriculum and is mandatory for becoming a competent professional taster. It's also one of the main reasons why the learning curve for wine involves a duration of time and a good deal of tasting practice. That said, to the detractors' point, are these variety descriptions consistent to the extent that they can be universally found, much less taught? The answer is … sort of.

Many descriptions of the classics include impact compounds found in a specific grape variety or family of grapes from which the wine in question was made. Examples would be pyrazines for Sauvignon Blanc and Cabernet Sauvignon-family red wines, or terpene/floral qualities for aromatic white grapes/wines such as Gewürztraminer, Muscat, and Viognier. Aromas and flavors from winemaking techniques, such as lees contact, malolactic fermentation-conversion, and the use of oak also come into play. There are over a dozen of these so-called impact compounds that delimit specific grapes and wines. It's imperative for students to learn them.

It's with structure and fruit ripeness and quality that the naysayers can have their day. Climate change continues to wreak havoc in vineyard regions around the globe. The rise in average temperature is causing the annual life cycle of vines to be pushed forward, with harvest now weeks earlier than it once was in many regions. More importantly, violent swings in weather patterns create drought conditions and destructive fires followed by heavy rains and flooding. No surprise that vintage variation now seems to be the rule and not the exception for many places, including some considered to be classic. Warmer temps also mean riper grapes, which results in higher alcohol in the bottle along with less natural acidity and the possible need for acidulation. Overripe and even stewed/cooked fruit also often occurs.

What does it all mean in regard to the descriptions I use for classic wines in the book, much less the way I write about and teach them? It means that going forward, the system needs to be more flexible than ever. I still believe these descriptions are relevant and important. They will continue to serve as valuable learning tools for some time, despite the fact that climate change will persist in altering the character of places and respective wines around the world.

In the end, there are times when I think the lexicon we use for teaching classic wines is like a huge stretch of ice floating in the Arctic. During my time in the business, the ice has begun to break apart with various bits—classic styles of wines--drifting away. What the *grapescape* will look like in 10 or 20 years has yet to be determined. In the meantime, we still need standards for teaching and examining students, and to be able to judge wine quality as professionals. Varietal wine descriptions will remain one of the most important facets of any wine curricula. Otherwise, we have little commonality with which to communicate about wine, one of life's most delightful, shared hallucinations.

1-9-23

19

MACH CORK SPEED

Last summer, an accident with a Prosecco cork forced cyclist Biniam Girmay to withdraw from the famed Giro d'Italia bicycle race. Biniam is from Eritrea and was the first Black African to win a stage of a grand tour cycling race when he beat Mathieu van der Poel in a sprint to the finish line to win the 10th stage. However, soon after finishing the race, things went south when Biniam enthusiastically opened a bottle of Prosecco to celebrate and ended up popping the cork into his left eye.

The cyclist was immediately taken to a local hospital where tests revealed a hemorrhage in his eye. The team doctor recommended he avoid further physical activity, and Girmay had to withdraw from the race. Turns out that Biniam wasn't the first to experience the wrath of an errant Prosecco cork on the same tour. The aforementioned van der Poel was struck in the neck by a flying cork after winning the opening stage of the race. However, after the Biniam incident, the race organizer RCS decided to alter the Prosecco protocol by handing stage winners open bottles, thus avoiding any further injuries.

Doing stupid or dangerous things with a bottle of sparkling wine probably coincides with the invention of the method used to preserve all the tiny bubbles in the bottle itself. Every year people like our buddy Biniam are injured—even killed—by flying Champagne corks. There's a good reason why. It's called the laws of physics.

Bottles of sparkling wine are under considerable pressure—somewhere between 70 and 120 pounds per square inch, depending on the kind of wine. This is greater than the air pressure in an average car tire. Which means that a sparkling wine cork, when released from the bottle, travels at great speed. According to an article in the *Washington Post*, a Champagne cork leaves a bottle at approximately 25 miles per hour.[1] However, recent studies have shown that the gases around the cork can achieve much greater velocities at nearly twice the speed of sound,[2] approximately 1,524 miles per hour. Not only that, but in certain circumstances in the microseconds after a bottle of Champagne is uncorked, a condition called "mach disk" can be created; a sort of standing wave often seen with supersonic jet engines. Gérard Liger-Belair, a professor of chemical physics at the University of Reims Champagne-Ardeche, was quoted saying, "the velocity of gases expelled from the bottleneck reaches almost Mach 2, twice the velocity of sound."

What does it all mean? A bottle of bubbly is not to be taken lightly, much less trifled with. And while this chapter wasn't intended to be an educational piece on wine service, some safety tips for opening a bottle of sparkling wine can only be useful. Here are some key points taken from the standards for Champagne service used by various sommelier organizations. Several include warnings about safety.

1. McIntyre, Dave. "Champagne: You don't need a reason to pop a cork." Washington Post, 12 June 2014, https://www.washingtonpost.com/lifestyle/food/Champagne-you-dont-need-a-reason-to-pop-a-cork/2014/06/11/5de178f4-f02d-11e3-9ebc-2ee6f81ed217_story.html. Accessed June 2024.
2. Mercer, Chris. "Popping a Champagne cork is rocket science, says study." Decanter, 16 November 2019. https://www.decanter.com/wine-news/Champagne-cork-popping-study-426794/. Accessed June 2024.

The proper serving temp for a bottle of sparkling wine is approximately 45 degrees F. Make sure to chill the bottle thoroughly before opening. If chilling a bottle in the fridge, allow for at least two hours, if not longer. You can use the freezer—but don't forget the bottle. Yes, we've all done it and it's messy. It reminds me of a marching band trip in college. Regrettable.

- If chilling the bottle in an ice bucket, make sure it's a 50-50 water-ice mixture. Otherwise, you'll be trying to jam the bottle into a bucket of ice.

- Above all, make sure the bottle is thoroughly and evenly chilled. This is important when you go to quick-chill a bottle that's room temperature (or cellar temperature) in an ice bucket with the top 30% of the bottle not submerged. Before opening, make sure the temp of the neck and bottom of the bottle are the same—as in both cold. If not, allow for more time in the ice bucket.

- When opening, use a cloth napkin or kitchen towel over the top of the bottle to prevent any messy accidents—unless that's the prime directive of the moment.

- <u>Never</u> take the cage off the bottle before removing the cork. If you insist on doing that, you are, in effect, holding a live tactical device.

- Also, <u>never</u> point the bottle at anyone when opening it. And for God's sake, don't point the bottle at yourself. Just ask Biniam Girmay about it.

- Cut the capsule underneath the cage with a blade of a corkscrew and discard.

- Place a cloth napkin on top of the cage, and then place your hand on top of the napkin. From there, do NOT take your hand off the top of the bottle until the cork is out.

- Hold the cage and cork as firmly as you can.

- Undo the wire cage by reaching underneath the napkin and twisting the small wire ring six times counterclockwise, all the while keeping your hand on top of the bottle.

- Remove the cork slowly by turning the bottom of the bottle and not the cork.

- When the cork is almost out, very gently push it to the side to let the excess CO_2 out of the bottle quietly. Yes, I know the lack of noise may not be festive, but opening a bottle quietly is much cooler than the opposite, which anyone can do. Even a professional cyclist. Ouch.

That's it. Opening a bottle of sparkling wine safely isn't easy. It takes practice. That's why people are paid to do it in restaurants and beyond, and why any server who wants to be hired in a decent restaurant should be able to demonstrate their ability to do it safely and properly.

Finally, I have to mention sabering Champagne, which involves taking a large knife or similar and hacking off the entire top of the bottle to open it. The following is my opinion and not shared by other colleagues. I believe that sabering a bottle is potentially dangerous and stupid. It's the wine version of chasing parked cars. That's because the person wielding the blade is trusting the structural integrity of the bottle is sound. And 99 out of 100 times it is. But when it isn't, the bottle explodes and various body parts get sliced up by shards of flying glass. Regardless, sabering Champagne remains popular in some circles. I'll take a pass.

Enjoyment of sparkling wine and Champagne will probably always include the lure of stupid and dangerous activities. Darwin warned us about that over 160 years ago. But I wonder if he enjoyed a glass of Champagne now and again. One can only hope.

3-13-23

20

STRONG WATER: A PERSONAL WINE MANIFESTO

Jamie Goode's *The Goode Guide to Wine: A Manifesto of Sorts* is literally a pocket-sized personal philosophy about wine, from the tasting experience to commercial vs. artisan wine and beyond. In the preface, Jamie states more than once that he fully expects the reader to disagree with some, if not many, of his opinions. In fact, he actually hopes the reader does:

"I hope the ideas presented here cause you to question, and perhaps in turn to frame your philosophy of wine."

With that, I will follow Goode's lead and present my own thoughts about wine. I'll also be quick to point out that I hope you read and disagree with some of what I have to say. If anything, it's because we sometimes learn quickly when faced with a concept with which we disagree, with the caveat that we also approach the new information with an open mind.

One last thing. It's important to note that I'm dropping anchor, so to speak, in April of 2023. Any of the following is subject to change in the future given the right experience or tasting the right wine.

GENERAL THOUGHTS

A bottle of wine always involves a two-part equation including the vineyard source and the winemaker.

The quality of the fruit always matters.

High-quality fruit is a prerequisite for making good wine.

The wrong winemaker can screw up top-quality fruit.

A skilled winemaker can make good wine with lesser quality fruit—but not much beyond.

Overripe and raisinated fruit and high alcohol levels in wine can distort or even obliterate any sense of place, or terroir.

Vintage is not universally important. There are classic wines, such as non-vintage Champagne and aged tawny Port, where vintage is secondary.

Most white wines are produced with the intention of being consumed within a year of release. Then vintage only matters as far as seeking out the youngest wine available.

WINE STYLES

My Mom's maxim applies here: it takes all types to fill up the freeways.

There's a market for any style of wine, from inexpensive and commercially produced wines to terroir-driven single domain bottlings.

Box wines, jug wines, canned wines, and wines in Tetra Pack are all relevant and important to our industry.

If our goal as professionals is to share the wine experience with others, we need better quality wines in every format.

ON TASTING

Because wine is fermented, it smells and tastes like other things—hence the sometimes-florid descriptions about fruit, spices, flowers, and more found in a glass of wine.

The aromas and flavors in wine are derived from volatile compounds, which are the product of fermentation.

We describe these compounds in a number of different ways, including the aforementioned fruit, herbs and spices, earth and mineral, and oak.

To accept use of some wine descriptors but not others is ludicrous.

Deductive tasting using a double-blind method is useful for training and various certifications.

Other methods of tasting are equally valid.

Identifying wine via blind tasting is an important part of the educational process. However, it is **not** the end-all or be-all of professional tasting.

There are well over 100,000 commercially produced wines every year. To expect someone to identify any wine via blind tasting is somewhere between ludicrous and moronic.

Arguably, the most important goal of tasting is to assess and analyze a wine in order to be able to *judge its quality*. Ultimately, that is what we as professionals are trained—and paid—to do.

We practice tasting so we can be silent internally and present to what's in the glass—literally, so we can internally see what's there.

Personal tolerances and biases in wine must be navigated and even compensated for when tasting for professional purposes.

One cannot hack being a professional taster.

Any meaningful competence requires consistent use of a tasting grid or system, repetition, training, coaching, and a duration of time.

One is arguably never a great taster but always in the process of learning more and improving their craft.

The legendary cellist Pablo Casals practiced daily into his 90s. He was once asked why he continued to practice. His answer: "Because I'm beginning to see some improvement." I to use him as a model in my tasting.

COMMUNICATING ABOUT WINE

We communicate about wine to the consumer by making the complex simpler without dumbing it down.

Wine has no inherent vocabulary. Over time we in the industry have begged, borrowed, and shamelessly stolen terms from other completely unrelated fields. Thus, the language of wine will always be a challenge.

TASTING NOTES

Tasting notes are a useful tool as well as a necessary evil.

Most tasting notes are reductive in that we pry apart various aspects of a wine and then describe them as best we can.

Any tasting note will always combine an objective description of a wine with one's personal subjective opinion.

There's an enormous range in tasting note styles, from acerbic laboratory text to pulp fiction.

Any tasting note that a broad audience can use lies somewhere in between.

The intended end user should dictate the style of the tasting note.

TEACHING TASTING

We teach examples of classic grapes and wines to establish standards for tasting and overall wine knowledge.

We also know that the nature of these so-classics is constantly evolving due to climate change, vintage variation, and changes/improvements in the vineyard and winery.

TERROIR, EARTH, AND MINERAL

Every vineyard has a unique microbiome, the population of bacteria, micro flora and fauna, and yeasts, both cerevisiae and others.

Fermentation includes the yeast population, bacteria, and microbiome from the vineyard soil and winery environment.

Even if a cultured yeast is used for fermentation, the microbiome of the vineyard and winery can still impact the finished wine, even in the presence of sulfur.

The combined influence of microbiomes from the vineyard soil and winery on fermentation helps create aromas and flavors in wine that are commonly described as mineral and earth.

As personal expertise increases, wines that reflect their place of origin tend to matter more.

Certain fine wines can only be made in very specific places.

Regions and vineyards that have produced wine for thousands of years seemed destined to do just that. In a certain context, they could be described as sacred spaces.

WINE QUALITY, BALANCE, AND TYPICITY

Wine quality is based on typicity and balance.

Typicity in any given wine is a quality based on aromatic and flavor characteristics and structural levels commonly found in other wines from the same place of origin and made from the same grape or blend of grapes.

Balance in wine is a harmony between the fruit and acid in all wines, and fruit, acid, and tannin in red wines. The use of new oak can also play a role in overall wine balance.

Tannin management can make or break the balance in red wine and, to a certain extent, determines quality.

To many consumers, "smooth" is the single most desired quality in a red wine.

Deliciousness is another important but somewhat subjective aspect of balance. It usually involves the interplay between fruit and structural elements, such as acidity and residual sugar, if present.

A well-made wine should resemble other classic examples of the same grape and from the same place. There are always exceptions.

Like many things in wine, oak-aging is about context.

If there is one maxim about oak usage in winemaking, it's this: the intensity of fruit in a wine must match the amount of new oak. Other-wise, the wine can easily be imbalanced and one-dimensional.

EVOLUTION OF A PALATE (SEE CHAPTER 44)

One's palate evolves over time.

There seems to be phases that one generally goes through over time in regards to tasting and preferred wines:

Phase I: wine as confection – fruity, slightly sweet white, pink, and red wines

Phase II: white wine with oak – Chardonnay and others

Phase III: red wine with oak and tannin – Cabernet Sauvignon and similar

Phase IV: red wines of subtlety and elegance – Pinot Noir and similar

Phase V: high-acid white wines with residual sugar – Riesling, Chenin Blanc, and others

Phase VI: any style of wine that's well-made and of high quality

WINE AND CONTEXT

There are three aspects to any tasting experience: the taster, the wine, and context.

Context is by far the most important aspect of the three. It can be defined as the who, what, when, where, and how a wine is tasted.

Change any part of the context in a tasting—be it the ambient temperature of the tasting space, the temperature of the wine, the glassware, the order of the wines being tasted, and more--and you alter the experience of the taster, sometimes dramatically.

Context means that communicating about the wine experience will always be imprecise because there are multiple variables.

With the exception of TCA and certain sulfur compounds, many of what we call "faults" in wine are contextual.

However, when a fault like Brett or VA dominates the character of a wine, the wine is flawed.

SUBJECTIVE VS. OBJECTIVE IN THE WINE EXPERIENCE

The wine experience will always be a combination of objective and subjective.

There are two primary ways of looking at the issue of objective vs. subjective in wine.

First, everything we experience in life is subjective—the product of our nervous system and brain.

Our connection to the physical universe is our five senses. Internally, we think using the same five senses.

Thus, everything we perceive, recognize, and remember is filtered through our internal senses.

In that way, everything in life is subjective to us.

Second, there are elements in wine that can be isolated and quantified in a lab. These elements are objective.

Other aspects of wine are filtered through personal experience and are more subjective in nature.

To a beginner, practically all of the tasting experience is subjective.

As time goes on and is experience gained, tasting becomes more objective.

There is little about wine that is subjective to an experienced professional.

GREAT WINES VS. GREAT WINE EXPERIENCES

Wines from "great" vintages tend to show intensity, concentration, and considerable tannin, if the wine in question is red.

More often than not, a high-quality wine from a so-called great vintage needs extended time in the cellar. If paired with a meal when young, the wine will tend to dominate the food.

Wines from so-called lesser vintages have intrinsic value.

If balanced and typical, a wine from a lesser/lighter vintage will prove to be more versatile with food.

Great wines shout while others whisper. There is more than enough room for both.

Great wines are usually prohibitive in cost, but so-called lesser wines can still potentially make for a great wine experience.

It's important to make the distinction between a great wine and a great wine experience.

A great wine is as implied: a prohibitively expensive and/or legendary bottle tasted at a trade event or via the cellar of a generous collector.

A great wine experience is where context, as in the people, place, and time, are just as important, if not more so, than the wine itself.

With some great wine experiences, the actual wine may not even matter.

NATURAL WINE

All winemaking is intervention. Period.

There is no one best style of wine or winemaking. To proclaim a specific kind of wine as the one "true" or "best" style is beyond ludicrous.

It's important to note that there are wines made *naturally* with minimal handling and minimal addition of sulfur by talented and experienced winemakers.

There are also "natural" wines, some so flawed they should never be commercially sold. The two should not be confused.

Practically all the most flawed wines I've ever tasted had one thing in common: they were natural wines.

As a category, natural wine needs standards and certifications.

Adopt an extreme position or viewpoint in wine--be it place, grape, or style--and the universe will be all too happy to immediately show you one or several exceptions.

NUMERICAL SCORES

The 100-point scoring system presupposes precision and objectivity in wine that has never existed—and never will.

While numerical scores may benefit the collector and drive sales in certain industry channels, they do consumers a considerable disservice.

Numerical scores are the industry's true unicorn.

THE SOMMELIER'S VIEWPOINT

There are many "windows" in the wine universe.

The sommelier's window is about hospitality and taking care of the guest with wine as part of a great dining experience.

Sommeliers find the right wine to serve in their restaurant tonight, and not a wine that will be ready to drink in five years.

Thus, sommeliers tend to judge wine quality and typicity in the time frame of *now* and not at some point in the future.

IN THE END

Wine is the great connector—it connects us to people and places like a few other things.

The shared pleasure of a bottle of wine is one of life's great gifts.

As sommeliers, we connect our guests to great wines and great wine experiences.

We in the industry are the benefactors of one of mankind's greatest achievements.

To me, it's humbling to smell and taste wine, an act that has been performed countless times over the last 7,000-plus years.

I'm grateful to have had a career in wine and to have had a chance to play the game.

A votre santé!

4-7-23

21

THE MUSIC-WINE
CONNECTION

Is there a connection between music and wine? I'm sometimes asked that question and feel qualified to answer it as I have two degrees in music as well as a 35-plus year career in wine. However, the answer isn't as simple as something inane like *Mozart is like Champagne*. For the record, I think Vivaldi and Prosecco are a better match. But the quick answer to the question is yes. There are more than a few connections between music and wine due to the multitude of parallels between the two fields. First, both are sensory-based. Both also have considerable depth in terms of their respective history, culture, sociology, philosophy, and even spirituality. But perhaps the most important connection between music and wine is how they make us think. How extensive training in either can create complex and refined patterns of thought not necessarily found in other endeavors.

I started playing the trumpet in fourth grade. Several years later, my first job in the restaurant business--bussing tables in a pancake house from 6:00 PM to 4:00 AM--helped pay for my first professional trumpet (see Chapters 1 and 2). I played in various groups, including concert bands, jazz bands, marching bands (true!), and orchestras from the time I was in grade school to my undergraduate days at the University of New Mexico, graduate school at the University of Michigan, and beyond. In other words, I played the trumpet from the time I was 12 until my mid-30s when I put the horn down.

After grad school, Carla and I moved to San Francisco, where I played with orchestras all over the Bay Area, as well as an extra with the San Francisco Opera Orchestra. I freelanced for over four years until the restaurant business and impending parenthood took over. Thus, music was—and has always been—a vital part of my career and life, and I can easily draw on my own experiences to explain the music-wine connection. To that point, there are many things from my musical training that helped with my wine career. In fact, I never would have passed the Master Sommelier examinations without my musical training. Here are some of the aspects that mapped over from music to wine.

SHUTTING THE WORLD OUT

Playing a musical instrument (or singing) requires immense focus. One's success ultimately depends on being able to shut the world out and concentrate singularly on playing, as well as what other musicians are playing if performing in an ensemble. Tasting also requires great focus and the ability to shut the world out in order to discover what's in the glass. I would suggest that both are a refined trance or altered state in a manner of speaking.

GAME DAY SKILLS

Game day skills mean the ability to bring one's best effort exactly when needed. The MS Exam is a series of three specialized auditions, as all are oral examinations. I'm convinced I would never have passed the exams if it weren't for the trumpet auditions I took from the time I was in junior high all the way to my years as a professional. As tough as the MS exam was, it wasn't nearly as intimidating as some of the auditions I took as a professional.

UNCONSCIOUS COMPETENCE

Competence in this context means unconscious competence with the ultimate goal of mastery. This is the so-called scale of competence that ranges from *unconscious incompetence* (I'm oblivious to the fact that I can't dance), to *conscious incompetence* (wow, I really suck at dancing), to *conscious competence* (I can dance, but I really have to work at it), to *unconscious competence* (wow, that person is an amazing dancer and they make it look so easy). Music and wine are both endeavors where this scale applies. In music, one translates written symbols on the page to hopefully refined sounds. To accomplish this, there are an untold number of processes, both conscious and unconscious, that must be followed before a single note is played.

With the trumpet, it's all about breathing. Specifically, the cycle of inhalation, exhalation, and the release of a note. It's a cycle that has to be practiced literally thousands of times to become consistent, especially under the duress of an audition or performance. With wine, one practices tasting using a grid in order to connect the dots and identify a specific grape variety, a style, a place, and even a particular year of production. This also requires repetition in the form of thousands of wines tasted to gain unconscious competence.

HEIGHTENED SENSORY ACUITY AND AN EXPANDED FIELD OF AWARENESS

This is perhaps the most important music-wine connection of all. How music and tasting affect the way we think. A musician in a professional orchestra is required to have a remarkable level of sensory acuity. I remember performing the Verdi Requiem one time with an orchestra of over a hundred musicians. Also on stage were several vocal soloists in front of the orchestra, a chorus of over 200 singers directly behind me, and a dozen off-stage brass players positioned hundreds of feet from the orchestra in the balcony of the concert hall. From moment to moment, I had to focus on everything going on around me, including my own part, watching the conductor, and listening to the other people in my section, as well as all the various instruments and singers around me. Every instant, I had to adjust the volume and timbre of my sound while playing my part in tune and in time with the rest of the trumpet section —and the rest of the orchestra. I can't tell you how I did this, or how any musician does it, for that matter. But I can tell you that performing at a high level requires one to keep an enormous number of things in their field of awareness, either simultaneously or in rapid sequence.

Wine tasting is much the same. In interviews I've done over the years with MS and MW colleagues about their tasting strategies, I've noticed one major pattern: smelling and tasting wine is a visual experience internally for practically everyone, and top tasters have unique and intricate ways of mentally organizing all the sensory information in a glass of wine. Like a musician, a professional taster can keep a great number of aromas and flavors as well as structural elements from a given wine in their field of awareness either simultaneously or in rapid sequence. And they do so using internal images and other visual patterns.

HEIGHTENED SENSORY AWARENESS

For most, visual is our dominant internal sense. Most of the human race thinks in pictures and movies. The accomplished musician goes one further by elevating auditory/sound in the form of listening and playing/singing to the level of internal sight. An experienced musician calibrates pitch, volume, and timbre with as much precision as a visual artist does with color, contrast, shade, and more. Likewise, a professional taster elevates smell and taste to the level of internal visual by identifying and calibrating all the aromas and flavors in the glass. For example, the character or quality of fruit in wine could be fresh, dried, cooked, stewed, or other. An experienced taster also calibrates the structural elements in wine in the form of the levels of acidity, alcohol, phenolic bitterness, and tannin. With that, I've heard many musicians describe their experience of music and/or playing as three-dimensional. Some tasters have also described their internal experience of wine as three-dimensional.

THE IMPORTANCE OF THEORY AND ACCUMULATED EXPERIENCE

It may sound esoteric, but a trumpeter playing in an orchestra has to know the difference between playing forte (loud) in a Mozart symphony vs. playing forte in a Mahler symphony. Even though both are marked identically on the page, they're completely different. In Mozart, the trumpet rarely plays above mezzo forte (medium-loud), even when the part is marked forte. This is because of the acoustical properties of the instruments of Mozart's time, a time when string instruments weren't capable of playing loud. And when trumpets were no more than extensions of a military fife and drum corps. However, the trumpet Mahler wrote for in his symphonies at the end of the 19th century was close to the instrument of today. He (Mahler) took full advantage of what the trumpet could do and wrote some of the greatest literature for the instrument. And when Mahler wrote forte—or fortissimo, he intended for trumpeters to play loud with the caveat that a good sound be used.

In wine, theory is always key. In blind tasting it's almost impossible for one to get to a conclusion such as "Spain, Tempranillo, Rioja Gran Reserva, 2011" without knowing that a classic style of Tempranillo from Spain comes from the Rioja region. Further, that Rioja as an appellation has a quality hierarchy of which Gran Reserva is the highest designation. It goes without saying that one also needs to know all the markers for the Tempranillo grape.

FINAL THOUGHTS

There are other parallels between music and wine, but I will leave you with this. Both tend to create passion and drive on the part of the individual pursuing a career. Both also require a willingness on the part of the student to spend a great deal of time practicing alone to improve skills, which includes the repetition of tedious and often boring things. Finally, music and wine are fields involving a high degree of aesthetics and beauty. In many ways, they are two of the greatest things our civilization has ever produced. Music, wine, and life: it's a wonderful combination.

10-15-13

22

WORDLESS WINES

Though it may surprise you, I've only been to Paris twice. Both times were on the same trip in the fall of 1987 when Carla and I went to Europe together for the first time. We stayed in the City of Lights at the beginning and end of our trek. Never having previously set foot on French soil, much less Paris, I utterly geeked out on art museums and cathedrals. Carla quickly had her fill of both, so we often split up for several hours at a time while I continued to gawk at incredible art in the Louvre, Musée d'Orsay, and other museums.

We also saw a myriad of Parisian sights together. One of the most memorable was Sainte Chapelle. If not familiar, Sainte Chapelle is a royal chapel built in the Gothic style. It's located in the medieval Palais de la Cité, which is on the island of Île de la Cité in the River Seine. The palais was the residence of the Kings of France until the 14th century. Sainte Chapelle was built to house precious Christian relics, including Christ's crown of thorns which Saint Louis had acquired. The chapel was constructed in just seven short years. It's filled with 15 stunning floor-to-ceiling stained glass windows over 45 feet tall. The panes comprise over a thousand biblical scenes from the Old and New Testaments, depicting the history of the world until the time when the relics were placed in the chapel.

I remember the day we saw Sainte Chapelle. It was a sunny fall afternoon with the leaves on the trees showing shades of yellow and gold. I recall stepping inside the chapel and immediately stopping in my tracks, completely stunned. The interplay of light filtering through the majestically tall windows was dazzling to the point of almost being overwhelming. Trying to describe it was impossible. Words simply failed.

Sometimes, words also fail with wine. To that point, I've spent the better part of the last three decades-plus trying to describe wine, both verbally and in written form. It's a journey that involves a long, sometimes painfully slow process of building skills with olfactory perception and memory. Also, using pattern recognition to connect the dots between impact compounds (a subset of the most important aromas and flavors), fruit character, and structure levels. It may sound like a lot, because it is. There is no hacking the process of becoming a professional taster. One is never a great taster but is always in the process of getting better at it.

Like many in the industry, my tasting notes are reductionist in nature. In other words, I break down a given wine into various components based on what it looks, smells, and tastes like. I learned this system over 30 years ago through the Court of Master Sommeliers and have used it countless times, both in an internal context when I think about and recall wines (which I do obsessively), and externally when tasting and taking notes.

Some complain about using a reductionist grid, saying it coldly dissects wine. However, using any tasting grid is better than the previous old-school philosophy of describing wines as "shy," "insipid," or "provocative." Regardless, one needs a shopping list of sorts to evaluate wine in a meaningful way. Otherwise, being consistent in assessing a broad range of different styles would be a constant and daunting challenge. Regular use of a tasting grid also helps to establish benchmarks so that future wines can be compared against a standard.

But as good as any reductionist grid is, there are times when it fails. Times when the combination of the wine in the bottle and context creates something that goes far beyond language. In this case, any attempt to describe what you're smelling and tasting–either verbally or in writing—becomes difficult, if not impossible.

One of these "wordless wines" immediately comes to mind: the 1990 Domaine Ponsot Clos de la Roche Grand Cru Cuvée Vieilles-Vignes. All great Red Burgundy is transcendent. Putting your nose in the glass is to be gently assaulted by a tsunami of aromas so complex it can be impossible to describe. The '90 Ponsot was just that. The experience reminded me of standing in the nave of St. Chapelle and being inundated by brilliantly faceted light in infinite shades and colors that changed constantly with the slightest shift in atmospheric light outside.

Likewise, when I smelled the Ponsot, the aromas changed every time I put my nose in the glass. The wine showed extraordinarily complex layers of fruit, spices, game, earth, and oak. The sum total shimmered like the surface of a quickly moving stream. Each time after I smelled and tasted the wine, I'd put the glass down, smile, shake my head, and utter a quiet but emphatic *wow*.

The wine also had remarkable depth and concentration without being heavy on the palate. In effect, it was weightless. I've come to think that most great wines are just that—weightless. They show great intensity and concentration without being heavy.

Scientists tell us that the left hemisphere of our brains specializes in reading, writing, speech, abstraction, and numbers. Regarding language, this area of our brain is where we put together concepts piecemeal by reading groups of individual words in sequence. The right, more ancient hemisphere of our brains perceives images, solves spatial problems, recognizes faces, and appreciates music. In thinking about the Ponsot Clos de la Roche, perhaps the overwhelming amount of sensory information presented to me in the moment confounded my left brain, forcing me to use my more ancient imaging/feeling right brain. Hence the difficulty in describing the wine.

There have been other wordless wine experiences over the years. Tasting five Goldkapsul Auslesen from the Saarburger Rausch vineyard made by the supremely talented Hanno Zilliken was like sipping five variations of ethereal nectar. A magnum of 61 Krug Champagne was a perfect yet indescribable combination of aged fruit, dried exotic flowers, and truffled earth gently cradled by delicate bubbles. Over a dozen of Steven Henschke's offerings tasted at the winery were a theme and variations on perfectly textured red wine made from old vine sources.

In the end, I know I'm not the first to sometimes struggle with words when it comes to describing what's in the glass. I won't be the last. In the future, there will be times—and wines–when words will fail. In a way, it reminds me of how wine makes for a good life. And to always be on the lookout for the next wordless wine.

5-2-22

PART FOUR

POTPOURRI

Potpourri is a term for a group of things used in lieu of words/phrases such as a lot, bunch, collection, mess, or a veritable smorgasbord. I could instead have called this section mélange or pastiche, but that might have put you, the reader, into a trance vs. keeping your interest to read on. Otherwise, as implied, the following section of the book is a series of chapters on unrelated topics that make up for a savory, complex, and hopefully interesting whole. Just like potpourri.

23

IL DISASTRO DEL CAFFÈ

In the restaurant business, there are certain times during the arc of a meal when things at the table have to happen fast—and they have to be right. In the beginning, when someone orders a cocktail or bottle of wine, it has to hit the table pronto. At the same time, if anyone at the table looks hungry, food of some kind (usually bread) has to arrive just as quickly lest a blood sugar crisis ensue. Bookending the meal, if coffee is ordered after the entrées are cleared, it needs to appear in short order. Finally, and this is important, once the check is requested, it needs to arrive within five minutes. No exceptions. No excuses.

Likewise, there are certain moments during the daily routine when things have to happen fast, and they have to work. For example, one's morning coffee. The process needs to be efficient and take into consideration the fact that the drug about to be administered is exactly what's lacking to make things work. Further, the lack of said stimulant can potentially create disaster scenarios like the one pictured above.

The tragedy occurred on the morning of February 20th, 2014. I only know that because the date is attached to the photo via my phone. Thank God for that. It helps reinforce my already shaky past timeline and murky memory. Otherwise, it was a Thursday. Or so Google tells me.

No doubt it was a cold, foggy winter morning in the rarely sunny Sunset District of San Francisco. At the time, I was still buying coffee beans, grinding them, and making single cups of coffee. Mind you, I'd been doing that for the better part of 30 years. And I didn't call it "pour-over." That's ludicrous. It's called using a Melita. And we don't need any stinking badges.

Usually, the process was simple. Heat the water, grind the coffee, and combine the two to create a dark, bilious, and magic liquid that revs the mind and boots up the mainframe. All this times two, as Carla also needed a cup. However, on this particular morning, my subconscious had other things in mind. It must have been watching Buster Keaton movies all night and decided to go rogue.

The first part, involving heating the water and grinding and loading the two Melita cones with coffee, was just ducky. But when I went to pour water, things completely went to hell in seconds. I somehow nicked my cup with the pot of hot water, knocking it over. It, in turn, hit Carla's cup, which also hit the counter. In seconds, steaming Joe and silty coffee grounds were all over the counter and dripping onto the floor. I'm sure I barked out a few well-chosen expletives. But then I just stood there and watched in resignation as the coffee and grounds went everywhere. It's funny how as one gets older, getting outraged or pissed off at personal failure simply isn't worth the effort.

But the moment was too disastrous not to photo document for future generations. Then it took the better part of 20 minutes to clean up, reset, and make coffee without further incident. At least I had the photo to prove how spectacular the failure was. Carla and my daughter Maria were both impressed.

We got our first Nespresso machine the year before. It was a gift of sorts for my being a guest sommelier at a Nespresso-sponsored dinner. We used it from time to time. But within weeks after the incident above, it became my go-to method for daily coffee. The lure of good espresso made with just the touch of a button was too much to resist, not to mention avoiding another coffee disaster.

We've used Nespresso ever since. Before anyone gets dangerously excited, we recycle all the used pods. The company makes it easy to do, providing recycling bags and free shipping via UPS. It should also be noted that new coffee pods are made from 80-percent recycled materials.

The most impressive thing about the Nespresso Gestalt is that it takes all the variables out of the coffee-making process. Variables like the quality of the coffee, the particular grind, and the amount of coffee to water needed. All of which combine to make or break the quality of a cup. It's like the screwcap in wine. There, only opposable digits are required to open the bottle. And there's no chance of TCA taint from a faulty cork. That is not to say TCA can't find its way into the wine from other sources. Sorry, too much information.

Back to stimulants. All this means that I can concoct a properly made double Cortado within several minutes of stumbling into the kitchen.

And that is a beautiful feat of technology. I just wish the same principle could be applied to other areas of my life. Perhaps that's what Marie Kondo has been trying to tell me all along. Maybe I should listen to her. Or at least invite her over for coffee.

5-13-22

24

LECHE

Yesterday, the half-gallon of milk Carla brought home from the store somehow fell over in the bag on the way and leaked a bit. However, the structural integrity of the plastic jug seemed no worse for the wear with the seal unbroken. When I opened the milk this morning, it smelled OK. Actually, it didn't smell like much at all. That should have been a sign.

I added a splash to my double espresso and then headed back to the office, pausing to turn on the AC as well as the overhead fan in the room. Then I took a sip of coffee. I paused. Frowned. It didn't taste bad —but it didn't taste like the usual. Sort of flat and metallic. That's my wine brain talking, mind you.

Then a variation of the shoulder angel/shoulder devil thing commenced. First, the stern, bitchy voice from being raised in a large, financially strapped Catholic family raised a bony finger and said:

"The milk is fine. Stop complaining and just drink your coffee. And

don't even think about tossing out the milk. That would be so wasteful."

I took another sip of coffee. It tasted worse. Then the other voice responded. The voice developed from years of being an adult who criticizes holy mother church at the drop of the pontiff's hat, which is called a miter, by the way. Which means it must be a meter tall. Anyway, this was my grownup voice's response:

"No, you're wrong. The coffee doesn't taste good, and the milk is bad. I'm going to toss it out and will replace it later today when I go shopping. And piss off, already."

No surprise that these two have never gotten along. If it were up to uptight Catholic voice, I'd still be going to mass every Sunday, which is as likely as a host of angels passing through the fold of a burrito. Meanwhile, my adult inside voice knows funky milk when it smells it. This is not a new thing. Even as kids, we knew when milk was headed to the petri dish stage and also when it was downright undrinkable. The funny thing was that we were lured to a bad carton of milk like moths to a flame, even to the point of having to share it with any other kids in the vicinity. "Here, smell this. It's really bad!"

As a kid, my family actually drank powdered milk for a time. Family finances and six little hungry Gaiser mouths to feed didn't allow for the consumption of regular milk. I well remember the smell and taste of powdered milk, not that far from the powdered baby formula Mom bought for my sister Annie when she was just a tot. One time, I came up with the brainy idea that you could add the butterfat back into powdered milk by heating a batch and melting actual butter in it. This must have been the same part of my brain that later came up with the squeegee with a long-handle window cleaning idea.

I went to the store and used all my spare change to buy two sticks of real butter. Then I went home and heated a small saucepan of just-mixed powdered milk. I added a stick of butter and stirred the brew over low heat. Eventually, the butter melted, leaving a pale yellow slick on the surface of the milk. When cooled, the combination tasted like... powdered milk with melted butter. So much for bad science.

In time, family finances improved to the extent that Mom could actually buy real milk again. She did so by the gallon. But with six kids, a gallon only made it around the dinner table once. The oldest three of us soon discovered that if you poured yourself a glass, drank half of it, and then repoured, you could get enough milk for dinner. The youngest three no doubt howled in protest.

Milk also reminds me of wine trips to Germany at a time when the concept of low-fat dairy didn't exist. If anything, it was the opposite, with milk so rich in butterfat it would be labeled as half-and-half here in the U.S. The cheeses, most made from unpasteurized milk, were so rich they were like savory ice cream. I think about hotel breakfasts in Germany. In particular, I remember breakfast at Hoffman's Weinstube in Bernkastel in the Mosel Valley. My tour group stayed there in the spring of 2000 and 2001. Hoffman's was a smallish hotel with maybe a dozen rooms and a restaurant and bar on the ground floor. Breakfast was served punctually at 7:00. Attendance wasn't optional. The proprietress was named Ursula. She could easily have been Frau Blücher's stunt double.

Every morning, Ursula put out a massive spread of sliced meats of every kind, cheeses, hard-boiled eggs, pastries, fruits, and preserves. There was coffee with milk, the latter having the consistency of heavy cream. The sliced meats were an assortment of head cheeses and other unrecognizable exotic sliced beasts that I quickly dubbed "church windows." The coffee was strong beyond belief.

As for coffee and dairy, my habits have changed over the years due to age and pseudo-health concerns. During college I only took my coffee black. At the time, I was buying fresh-roasted whole bean French Roast by the pound. The beans looked like little oily dark-as-night beetles, and the coffee was like black bile that shimmered with caffeine. I could drink an entire pot of it solo at night and still manage to sleep. How was that even possible?

As time went on, half-and-half in strong coffee became the routine. But at some point, my GP sounded the high cholesterol alarm and I had to switch to whole milk. I also cut out grilled cheese sandwiches at that point, but not the chips. When that didn't work, I moved to 2% milk. I've been there ever since. I utterly (udderly) refuse to go to 1%. It tastes like the paste we used to eat as kids mixed with water. Perish the thought of non-fat milk. The stuff is hideous.

Back to that morning. One final tragic sip and the coffee got the heave-ho. I remade a double espresso and used some of Carla's half-and-half. So the adult voice won, and the uptight Catholic voice got its comeuppance, at least for the time being. Otherwise, I'll pick up some milk when I'm shopping this afternoon for dinner. Because what's coffee without leche?

6-8-22

25

MY LIFE IS CORKED

When I was in junior high, there was a song called "Love Is All Around" by a group called the Troggs. I think it might even have been the song that was playing during my first slow dance, which at the time was more like two youngsters putting their hands on each other's shoulders and swaying back and forth to the music without making further physical contact or falling down. For boys, it was like a victory lap taken by a dog that somehow managed to catch a car with shiny hubcaps. For girls, it must have been exciting but also unnerving to be so close to a sweaty, feral human belonging to the opposite camp. Definitely the dogs and shiny hubcaps thing.

Thinking about it now, there are more things all around than just love. One of them is TCA or 2,4,6 trichloroanisole. It's a chemical compound called corkiness that results when certain kinds of mold combine with chlorine-derived substances. The result smells musty like wet concrete, old books and magazines, and practically every bag of so-called baby carrots.

The dark side of TCA occurs when it gets into cork products, specifically wine corks. With the human threshold to TCA as sensitive as six parts per trillion, TCA wreaks havoc on cork-finished wines, tainting and ruining millions of bottles a year. More than a decade ago, the cork industry, mostly based in Portugal, was under fire for rampant cork taint. Turns out that TCA taint was coming from using chlorine to bleach the corks at production plants. Hydrogen peroxide quickly replaced chlorine and TCA incidence decreased. However, it turns out that most TCA that forms on cork does so before the raw cork bark even arrives at a processing plant.

New storage and shipping protocols were introduced, and TCA numbers continued to decline. Using gas chromatography testing on cork batches to detect TCA also helped with quality control. However, it wasn't until the last couple of years that technologies were developed by the top cork producers to remove TCA from corks once formed.

Aside from tainted wine corks and mal vino, TCA is everywhere in the environment. A stroll past a rack of belts in a Walgreens can be like bouncing off a force field of TCA. Strolling in the park where the flower beds littered with bark chips have just been watered is to experience a new high of TCA. Then there's a restaurant where the floor was mopped with mop water kept from the night before.

I've been in corked cabs before and had corked bánh mì sandwiches with shredded carrots as the culprit. Even the tap water here in Rio Rancho sometimes has the double whammy of TCA and H2S (hydrogen sulfide). The water bottle I use at night on the bedside table sometimes reeks of corkiness from water taken from the fridge that's supposedly filtered.

As I write this, I'm in LA doing events for a client. This morning, I had breakfast in the restaurant downstairs. I left the AC on while I was gone, and when I returned to my room and opened the door, I walked into a waft of musty TCA. "Oh, jeez", I said. Actually, I said something much stronger.

So, while love may be all around, it's musty-ass TCA that surrounds us and inundates the environment. Sweaters can be corked. Carpeting gets corked. Unwashed dogs can probably get corked in the right circumstances. And if you live in a warm subtropical climate, your kids would probably get corked if they stayed outside long enough. There seems to be no getting away from TCA. It's everywhere. One might as well try to find a car with shiny hubcaps. Or at least a girl who's willing to dance.

10-27-22

26

THREE COWS

At some point in the past, I read a piece about the Marginal Utility Theory. It supposedly has to do with economics. The article explained the theory as follows: Imagine you have two farmers. Farmer A has three cows. Farmer B has 100 cows. If you give farmer A another cow, it's a big deal. After all, you've just increased his herd by 33%. But if you give farmer B another cow, it doesn't mean much because you've only increased his herd by a measly 1%. The bottom line is that the value of something can be relevant to the recipient. At least, that's the way I interpret it.

I witnessed the theory in action recently during a shopping trip to the local Albertsons. On that particular day, Maria, Patrick, and I had gone shopping for various basic victuals. We had already loaded up the belt at one of the checkout lines when a kid walked up behind me. He had a couple of Christmas cards and a coffee mug in hand. I asked him if that was all he had. He answered yes, and I immediately told him to get in front of us. He did, thanking me in a snucky voice.

The kid got in front of Maria and Patrick and then put the mug and cards on the belt. He was 10 or 11 years old and definitely on the nerdy side. He also wore a bulky winter jacket, jeans, and running shoes. I noted the shoes because I looked down to discover that his feet were huge—close to the same size as mine. He would easily be over six feet tall when he grew into them. Or forever be relegated to looking like a capital "L."

When it was his turn, the kid told the woman who was our checker that he only had about $20 and that he hoped it would be enough to cover the purchase. At that point, Maria turned to me and silently mouthed that he had a bad cold—and maybe not enough money. I told her we would cover the difference.

After the checker rang up the mug and cards, the kid pulled a piggy bank out of his jacket. And not just any piggy bank. It was in the shape of the BB-8 droid from the latest rash of Star Wars movies. As he went to take the rubber stopper out of the bottom, I could hear coins rattling around. Maria and I quickly exchanged one of those silent secret ninja looks that translates as "This does not look good." Sure enough, the kid was a couple of bucks short. Maria turned to me again and said, "I got this." She then told the kid not to worry and that she would take care of it. She quickly pulled out her ATM card and paid for the transaction. The kid was a bit taken aback but visibly grateful. He thanked her profusely. Then he leaned over, thanked me, and wished the three of us a Merry Christmas. And then he left.

As the checker rang up our goods, she thanked us for helping the kid out, saying it was a generous thing to do. I said something to the effect of "Hey, it's Christmas." But I was also glad Maria had helped the kid out. I'm sure the recipients, probably family members, appreciated the gifts. And he'll probably remember it too. Three cows.

The three cows thing comes to mind every time I'm presented with a check in a restaurant, specifically in regards to the tip. Over the years, I've made it a habit to tip at least 20%--more if the service is exceptional. If anything, because the person waiting on us is the essence of the three cow farmer. Schlepping food for a living is hard work regardless of where you do it, be it a diner or a three-star Michelin restaurant. You're stuck between a rock and a hard place as a server, specifically between all the pirates in the kitchen and the paying customers at the table. With the pandemic, the dynamics of both have changed dramatically—and not for the better.

With so many places being shuttered during lockdown, countless industry pros had to throw in the towel and look for work in another unrelated field, leaving a monumental dearth of experienced people working both the front and back of the house. Gone are the pirates in the kitchen who beforehand could crank out consistent plates of good food. They've been replaced by staff with a fraction of the experience. No surprise that in the last couple of years, food generally takes longer to get out of the kitchen. When it does, it can be inconsistent.

As for the front of the house, inexperience has also been the name of the game. A couple of days after the Albertson's incident, the four of us had dinner at a popular Italian joint. As we were munching on apps and yakking away, I watched surreptitiously as what looked to be a manager-type struggled to open a bottle of wine at a four-top. It was like her maiden voyage with a waiter's friend corkscrew, and the trip was not going well. She managed to make every possible mistake opening and serving the wine including breaking the cork and dripping wine on the table multiple times. She also reached across the table in front of everyone.

On the other side, there's the paying public, some of whom completely lost their dining chops and manners during lockdown. Rude and non-tipping customers are now more prevalent than ever. However, our server that night, named Max, was a pro. He definitely had skills. We thanked him for his good service and wished him happy holidays. I also threw in another cow by tipping him over 25%.

In the end, I may not believe in karma, but I do hold stock in the idea that "what goes around comes around." Handing out an extra cow is needed now more than ever. When in doubt—and when you can—give them another cow. You'll be glad you did. They will, too. Moo.

12-29-22

27

VIN BLANC

"Whenever life begins to crush me, I know I can rely on Bandol, garlic, and Mozart."

— JIM HARRISON

I just finished rereading the late Jim Harrison's last book called "A Really Big Lunch." If not familiar, Harrison was a prolific writer of poetry and prose, including the much-lauded trio of novellas called *Legends of the Fall*. He was also a raging gourmand with an enormous appetite not unlike the fabled Gargantuan of Rabelaisian fame. I don't make that statement lightly. Harrison was obsessed with good food and wine. He made no bones about drinking two bottles of Bandol Rouge a day. He never bothered with conventional wine glasses, instead opting for a huge tumbler and 12-ounce pours that he "gulped."

What's striking about revisiting the book is Harrison's ADHD, which was significant. Reading his text is like being shoved into a cranial pinball machine and being smacked about with at least a half-dozen topics on every page, but all covered with great elan and cleverness. To that point, Jim was an astute observer of the human condition and a brutal social critic. He spared no one, including himself.

Food and wine take center stage throughout the book. Even though the topics of more than three dozen essays vary from politics to the world going to hell in a handbasket, Harrison can't resist the lure of what he calls "vivid" eating. His descriptions range from hunting quail at his Arizona ranch to making bear posole at his cabin in Montana to any number of ways of preparing tripe. There's also no shortage of descriptions of dozens of meals enjoyed at high-end restaurants in France and beyond. The book's centerpiece--and title essay--describe a certain lunch in 2003 at a French restaurant owned by Harrison's favorite chef, Marc Meneau. In a marathon eight-hour session (with breaks, of course), Harrison and eleven others, including actor Gerard Depardieu, dined on 37 courses washed down by over 15 legendary French wines, some dating back to the 1950s.

If you think 37 courses of food is the stuff of excess, you would be right. Hard to argue with that. It's also hard to believe anyone was still alive the next day. This is French cooking, after all, where using butter, cream, and any other possible source of fat is the norm and not the exception. Harrison then chronicles how he wandered around Paris for hours the day after in a food coma. But then he found himself peckish by dinnertime, needing to stop at one of his favorite bistros before boarding a red-eye flight back to New York.

Harrison's views on politics—and everything else, for that matter—were strong water. No minced words, no middle ground. He hated the George W. Bush administration vehemently, saying it drove him to eat, drink, and smoke to excess—which he already did. His opinions on wine were just as strong. To him, good wine had to be red—the color of blood.

"The great north from which I emerge demands a sanguine liquid. White snow calls out for red wine, not the white spritzers of lisping

socialites, the same people who shun chicken thighs in favor of charac-terless breasts and ban smoking in taverns. In these days, it is easy indeed to become fatigued with white people, white houses, and white rental cars."

No surprise that Jim was a devotee of the importer Kermit Lynch, the latter responsible for putting dozens of French wines—mostly red--on the international map. Domaine Tempier, one of Lynch's discoveries, was an obsession with Harrison. White wines were a mere placeholder in his universe, only to be tolerated if red wine was unavailable—or a certain situation demanded it. Ultimately, he had to opt for white wine after being diagnosed with type two diabetes when *"two bottles of red wine a day became inappropriate, a euphemism of course. One bottle a day is possible with a proper morning walk with the dogs or rowing a drift boat for four hours in a fairly heavy current."*

Harrison is not the first I've come across who dismissed the white wine category outright. Conversely, some profess not to drink red wine because it gives them headaches. But the same people rarely bother to connect the dots between over-indulgence and said headaches. The culprit could be any number of things, including histamines and tannin in the wine or dehydration. There's also such a thing as too much wine.

In truth, everyone's sensitivity—or lack thereof—to the structural elements in wine (acidity, alcohol, and tannin) is different. Some crave white wines with insanely high levels of acidity, such that they could be used to make ceviche. These acid freaks probably drank the vinai-grette remnants right out of the salad bowl as kids. Others, like the monster truck pull experience from the tannins of a just-released Napa Cabernet. The same wine might cause another's face to implode.

I would be remiss if I didn't mention context at this point. It trumps everything. A particular bottle sipped during a gorgeous sunset on a first date that, over time, becomes a married couple's perennial favorite wine. Or any number of first wine experiences enjoyed while in an exotic location. Then there was the guy who was a regular when I bartended in the 80s at a now-defunct seafood/oyster place in the financial district of the City. He always wore a pink cashmere sweater and drank nothing but White Zinfandel. He once told me that he didn't care for the wine so much as he wanted to drink something that matched the color of his sweater. I should also mention that he added Sweet N' Low to his White Zinfandel.

I can't imagine not drinking white wine. It's a necessary part of the vinous spectrum; the Yin to the Yang of red wine, the day to the night, the Abbott to Costello, etc. More often than not, white wines are a much more precise lens of a place compared to their red counterparts, where high alcohol, tannin, and new oak often muddy things. In particular, I'm a fan of unoaked, high-acid, and mineral-driven European whites, from Sancerre to Chablis to Pinot Bianco to Assyrtiko. Riesling is a favorite. Spätlese (late harvest) Riesling from Germany is literally my sweet spot. I think Riesling is transcendent and transparent. It offers a pristine representation of a vineyard and its microclimate like few other wines. Certain Rieslings also tend to be lower in alcohol. Combined with high acidity, it makes them a chameleon with food, matching well with just about anything aside from red meat or live game.

Age also matters. Not wine-age, but carbon-dating our own world-weary carcasses. Specifically, higher alcohol levels, tannins, and histamines in red wines are more challenging to metabolize as we get older. Not to mention that some form of protein usually accompanies red wines at the table with fat and salt on the side. Less red meat over time usually means less red wine. Perhaps that's not a bad thing. One can always make exceptions.

In the end, it's often said that a picture is worth a thousand words. That's definitely true with Harrison. In his later years, he resembled Pressed Rat and Warthog of 60s rock lyrics fame. The decades of hard living, chain-smoking, and gargantuan eating and drinking eventually took their toll. First, diabetes and then several bouts of gout. In the end, he died of a heart attack on March 26, 2016, in Patagonia, Arizona.

Sometimes I wonder about Harrison's life and his idea of "living vividly." Is it better to play it safe than exit stage left at a younger age? I'm not sure, but there must be some sort of middle ground. Whatever it is, I'm pursuing it. And I'll keep drinking white wine while I'm at it.

8-9-22

PART FIVE

TALES OF THE SOMMELIER

During the first five years we lived in the City, I attempted to carve out a career as a freelance classical trumpet player. While I did manage to secure some major gigs, like playing with the San Francisco Opera Orchestra as an extra and playing for the pope, there was never enough money in it to pay the bills. Hence, my return to the restaurant business was inevitable. I spent five years bartending at various restaurants. Then, in the fall of 1989, my friend John Cunin asked me to be part of the opening crew for his new restaurant called Cypress Club. I would be helping run the beverage program and working the floor as a full-time sommelier.

It was an incredible opportunity, and I'll always be grateful to John for it. However, the long hours and demands of the new job meant I wouldn't have time to play the trumpet. Faced with the decision to pursue a new career in wine or keep grinding it out on the horn, I chose the former. It was definitely the right move.

The Cypress Club opened in December of 1990, just weeks before the holidays. The combination of Chicago-based Jordan Mosier's fantastical *Alice in Wonderland* design and Chef Cory Shreiber's innovative cooking was magical. For the next 18-24 months, Cypress Club would be the hottest restaurant in the City. As expected, the place was insanely busy, and my work life for the first year and beyond was a minimum of 60 hours a week. Somehow, I also managed to attend trade tastings and events as well as tastings with my MS study group. The latter culminated in my passing the MS exam in March of 1992. In between, life was a blur with countless hours of dealing with inventory, carrying cases of wine up and downstairs, and working the floor.

The Cypress Club turned out to be my last restaurant job. I left in the spring of 1993 for a short stint with a local distributor and then worked at Heitz Cellar in Napa Valley. But I still have many memories of working the floor as a sommelier. This section of the book includes a few favorites, along with a couple of restaurant-wine-related pieces.

28

DEALING WITH WINE IN RESTAURANTS

Recently, I had a lengthy phone conversation with a friend who's not in the wine industry. During our chat he happened to mention how difficult it was to get a good bottle of wine in a restaurant. My reaction was somewhere between "No way" and "Seriously?" I was surprised, given that he dines out regularly and knows more than a bit about wine. After a few more questions, it quickly became apparent that his comfort level with wine in restaurants wasn't there. Dealing with a sommelier or huge wine list was a major challenge for him.

He's not alone. Dealing with what I call "wine ballet," or "being handed the wine list in front of my friends/colleagues/future ex-girlfriend," is a source of major stress for practically anyone. I wouldn't quite put it up there with the fear of public speaking, which, according to some sources, is even greater than the fear of death (tough audience, no doubt). But being put on the spot with a wine list the size of the Gutenberg Bible can definitely cause anxiety. No surprise that my friend didn't believe me when I told him it was no big deal. To help, I gave him my own strategy on how to get a good bottle from any wine list. Then I promised him I'd share it with all my closest friends. Here it is.

PRELUDE

There are some things you should know before you darken any restaurant's door, including the following:

a. Know the style of wine you like to drink. Go into a restaurant armed with the knowledge that, "I like a red wine with soft tannins like a Pinot Noir." Or "I really like big, oaky Cabernets that remind me of a monster truck pull."

b. Also, know what styles of wines you don't like, which is arguably more important than knowing what you do like. If you absolutely loathe oaky wines or break out in hives if the alcohol in a red wine gets to be over 15%, be sure to share that information when appropriate.

c. Have a couple of examples of wines you've enjoyed in the past that can be used as points of reference. It will be useful to have some wines in mind that you like and can be used in discussions with a server or a sommelier.

d. Price: know how much you want to spend for a bottle within $15-$20. Wine prices on restaurant lists can vary dramatically, but chances are you already have a good idea of how much you're willing to spend on a given dining excursion.

THE MAIN EVENT

Now you're ready to go. You've just entered the restaurant with the man/woman of your dreams. When the hostess races you both across the dining room, seats you next to the kitchen, and gives you one of those "adios amigo" smiles before racing off, leaving the glassware on the table spinning, don't panic. Keep breathing. Feel good. Feel confident. It's going to be alright.

a. The wine list: as you pick up the wine list, head to any section and check out the pricing. Spot the highest price you can find and the lowest price as well. Drag those to your mental trash bin and discard.

b. Find the average price: get a quick eyeball average of where most of the wines are priced. The average bottle price could be anywhere between $40 and $150, depending on the location and style of the restaurant. After all, there's a huge difference between a corner bistro and The French Laundry in terms of the cost of operations, infrastructure, and the rest. You should also know that restaurants do NOT make money by selling food alone but only manage to survive and hopefully thrive by selling alcoholic beverages.

c. Find the sweet spot: set your sights on the 50-60% range of the restaurant's pricing scheme. That's usually where the best values are, and that, mein liebchen, is your sweet spot.

d. Your server: when your server arrives and asks if you'd like wine with dinner, respond with something like the following:

"You know, this is a really good list. I'd like to talk to the sommelier or wine buyer if they're available."

e. If the sommelier or buyer is available, that's great. Hopefully, they will be available to chat in short order. Once they make an appearance at your table, be sure to relay pertinent information to them, as mentioned above:

1. *"This is a style of wine I really like."*
2. *"I really don't like X kind of wine."*
3. *"Here are some wines I've enjoyed in the past. What do you have that's similar?"*

f. Pricing: *"I'd like to spend $50-$60 on a bottle,"* or *"Please suggest a wine you really like for under $85."*

Be specific about your price range, but also keep in mind that part of their job is to sell. That means they will probably start in your price range and then suggest something a bit more expensive. Don't be put off. If their suggestion makes sense in terms of your personal favorite wine style--and it's still within your budget, consider it. However, if their suggestion is hideously expensive (meaning they either didn't listen to you or they're completely clueless), respond politely with something like:

"You know, that's really not what I had in mind. Could you please make a recommendation in the X price range?"

Likewise, if their suggestion is too obscure, don't hesitate to ask about the wine. Pacherenc du Vic-Bihl, anyone? Good questions to ask about any recommendation would include the sweetness/dryness level for any style of wine, or the amount of tannin and oak if it's a red wine recommendation. If the wine is being poured by the glass, by all means, ask to taste it. Regardless, ask yourself if their recommendation fits your favorite personal wine profile. If not, don't hesitate to ask for something closer in style, such as a wine with less tannin and/or oak.

Discourse: a bit of back and forth is always good. The magic combination of your likes, dislikes, and desired price range should be more than enough info for practically anyone to help you get the right bottle.

CODA: MAGIC QUESTIONS

If in doubt, ask the following. You can always feel free to skip everything above and head straight to these.

"What are your favorite values on the list?"

"Is there anything you've just gotten in that you really like and think is a must-try?"

"Is there anything you're pouring by the glass that you really like and think is a great value?"

If you're speaking to the buyer-sommelier, chances are they will get dangerously excited at this point--or they should be checked for a pulse. This is the moment every sommelier dreams about. The moment when someone is asking their opinion about the coolest wines on the list that they have toiled countless hours to put together. What more could they want? Odds are they will blurt out the best/coolest/greatest/most amazing wine within nano-seconds of the question leaving your mouth. They may even get all verklempt on you. This is how it should be. If the wine is being poured from the glass, once again, ask to taste it. Otherwise, if the price is right, give it a spin. And if you really like their recommendation, be sure to let her or him know it, and even throw a bit of cash their way. It's always greatly appreciated.

5-23-19

29

LE BALLET TRAGIQUE DU VIN
(TRAGIC WINE BALLET)

"When the wagon of love breaks down under the baggage of life."

The process of opening a bottle of still or sparkling wine is straightforward. At least it should be. However, there's only one way to do it correctly, with minor variations depending on the style of service in a particular restaurant. Most of the time, it's done slightly wrong in the form of minor details left out, which don't offend and usually go unnoticed. These are the venial sins of the wine service confessional, if you will. Then there are the tragic errors, the cardinal sins, where even the most inexperienced diner may sit up and take notice while other, more informed, denizens of the dining room are alarmed, offended, or even possibly maimed. These catastrophic errors are the stuff of legend. This is the story of one dinner where the sommelier committed not one but three errors. The name of the restaurant and those involved have been changed to protect the record.

PRELUDE

Some years ago, I was in England working with the flavor develop-ment team of Frito-Lay International, the Willy Wonka division of the world's largest snack foods company. I worked with the UK team all afternoon on food and wine pairing combinations with an eye on creating a line of wine-friendly snacks. We had a productive session, and the six of us headed out to dinner in the best of spirits. My client had made a reservation at a small, well-known restaurant on the Thames in the countryside near Reading. He assured me it was the best restaurant in the region and had a great wine list.

I: Champagne service is not weapons training

After being seated, my client—and the host for the evening—suggested we order a bottle of Champagne to celebrate the occasion. A young, tall, red-haired lad appeared momentarily at the table and handed me a huge leather-bound tome that was the wine list. The list was comprehensive, with considerable depth in most major European wine regions. I scanned the Champagne section and chose a bottle of non-vintage rosé from a small grower-producer house. Order taken, the lad returned in a few minutes with Champagne flutes and the bottle of pink bubbly.

After presenting the bottle to me, he talked non-stop about the weather, the menu, and that evening's specials. He also undid the tab on the bottle and removed most of the capsule, accomplished with a single bold tearing motion (dwarf bullfighting came to mind). Without missing a beat, he undid the wire cage and put it in his pocket.

Afterward, he kept talking with the unprotected and very naked cork, pointing at us, at other guests, and then back at us again. I considered ducking under the table more than once but thought better of it, lest my colleagues believe I was overly dramatic. Finally, after threatening the entire dining room with the primed bottle, he reached for the cork with a grandiose gesture and promptly lost it with a spectacular and deafening BLAM. The cork rocketed out of the bottle and bounced off the ceiling, leaving a sizable dent before returning to the terra firma of our table and ricocheting onto the floor out of sight. The explosion was accompanied by the inevitable gusher of pink fizzy wine splattering over the lad's hands and onto the carpeting. A few moments of stunned silence ensued. Then Champagne guy mumbled something like, "Uh, Happy New Year," before pouring the bottle around the table without further ado.

The sin: losing control of a Champagne cork.

Consider safety first. A bottle of bubbly is under as much as 90 pounds per square inch pressure— more than in car tires. Opening a bottle is not to be taken lightly, as people are injured or even killed every year from errant Champagne corks. Safety, again, is the bottom line. Unless you've just won a Formula 1 race or you're launching the Queen Mary, opening the bottle quietly and safely is the prime directive. The overly zealous lad should have placed a folded serviette (cloth napkin) over the top of the bottle BEFORE loosening the cage. Then, with a firm grip over the napkin and top of the bottle, he should have loosened— but NOT taken off—the cage, removing the cage and cork at the same time as quietly as possible. Spewing wine, which we were paying for, is also not an option, and it gives yet another reason to open the bottle with a serviette draped over the top.

II: Did you want some too?

After Champagne guy left the table, we quickly regained our composure and sipped the bubbly. As everyone looked over the menu, I ordered a bottle of Premier Cru Chablis for the starter course from our waitress. Champagne guy was not to be found, so she brought the bottle to the table. She, too, was remarkably chatty but managed to get the cork out without incident. After opening the bottle, she asked if I would like to taste the wine. I said yes and then she proceeded to cheerfully pour me over half a glass. I grabbed my glass with the sturdy grip used by pirates for a daily ration of grog and rotated it slowly so as not to hose down my fellow diners. I took a sip and found it was delicious.

She smiled and proceeded to over-pour for the other guests. But she also ran out of wine before she got to the last person at the table, who also happened to be the host—the same host who would be picking up the check. To reiterate, she didn't make it around a table of six with a full bottle of wine, which is not easy to do. Much to her credit, she smiled and asked if we would like a second bottle. We politely refused, and once she left the table, several of us chipped in to make sure our host got some Chablis to accompany his appetizer.

The sin: running out of wine before you make it around the table is inexcusable.

Other than dropping the bottle on the floor or pouring wine on a guest at the table, nothing is tackier than running out of wine before you make it back to the host. It doesn't matter if it's a 12-top and the host is so clueless or cheap to only have ordered a single 750 ml bottle for the table. The sommelier or server should easily be able to make it around the table and pour off the bottle when serving the host, who incidentally should always be served last. If in doubt, massively under-pour everyone's glasses but never, EVER run out of wine.

III: The body was on the floor when I got here

After the appetizers were cleared, I ordered an older vintage of Rioja Gran Reserva to be served with the entrees. Then, I excused myself and went to the men's room. In my absence, the host informed the Champagne guy, who had reappeared, that I was a Master Sommelier. Probably not a good move. After I returned to the table, the lad showed up with the bottle of Rioja. Gone now was the youthful bravado that accompanied the Champagne incident. In its place was a serious case of nerves. The cork was removed without injury, but the dripping began immediately with his pouring a taste for me. After I approved the wine, he went around the table, serving everyone but leaving an almost perfect uninterrupted ring of red drips and splashes between place settings. By the time he made it back to me with the bottle, the tabletop looked like a crime scene. After an uncomfortable eternity, he finished pouring, set the bottle down firmly, and left the table visibly shaken. Everyone looked at the tabletop for many long moments and then stared at me. I shrugged and said, "Well, I guess I'll always have a job."

The sin: not using a serviette when pouring wine.

The fix: This one's a no-brainer. A serviette must always be used to prevent drips whenever serving wine. Otherwise, get out the yellow crime scene tape or a damp mop. Or both.

3/10/2012

30

VINOUS INTERRUPTUS

My reward for passing the Master Sommelier exam in March of 1992 was to work Sunday brunch two days later. It wasn't punishment; it was just how the schedule worked out. I wasn't about to pass the shift on to the other two sommeliers, who were good friends. To be honest, they would have refused to work it—and rightly so.

Several months later, on a Friday night, I had the first of many seminal sommelier moments, or reality checks, to be more precise. There I was on the floor wearing my shiny new gold and burgundy MS pin, feeling somewhere between Austin Powers and James Bond with a little Mr. Bean thrown in for gravitas. One of the first tables in the early seating was a four-top with two couples. After they had some time to settle in with the menu and wine list, I approached the table and asked the host with the list if he had any questions or needed a suggestion. He asked for a few minutes to look over the list.

When I returned to the table, he handed me the list and said with the utmost confidence, "We'll have the such-and-such old vines, Zinfandel." The wine in question was a seriously tannic red from a top Zinfandel producer in Sonoma County. We carried several of the winery's single-vineyard Zinfandels and only received a scant two-case allocation of the wine in question. It always sold out quickly. Our nickname for the wine was "Death Star" because of its high tannin level that really needed a decade or more of aging to resolve. Unfortunately, our prime directive from the owner was to move inventory, so that wouldn't happen.

"Just curious," I asked the host, "what will you be enjoying for dinner?" He responded by saying they would start by sharing a dozen oysters on the half shell, and then two of them were having the salmon in parchment while the other two had settled on sautéed local Petrale Sole. Immediately, all the sommelier alarms in my head went off at over 100 decibels. The combination of a tannic red with oysters and delicate fish was like a train looking for a wreck. I quickly went into triage mode and tried to talk the host out of the wine in every possible way by saying things like:

"Great choice. I tasted that wine recently, and it's a bit tight and fairly tannic. So, we might look at a delicious aromatic white to go with the salmon and Petrale instead."

Or

"Wow, that's a great Zinfandel. Someone last night enjoyed it with the chef's braised short ribs. You might consider that instead of the oysters and salmon."

Or

"A single bottle of Death Star has been known to level an entire village. I'm not sure we're licensed for it or have the proper safety equipment to administer it."

Just kidding about the last one. However, try as I might, I could not dissuade him from ordering the newly released vintage of Death

Star. "You don't understand," he said, "this is our favorite wine, and it's nearly impossible to find. We rarely get to enjoy it." I smiled and politely said, "Of course. I'll bring it right away and decant it for you." Visions of '50s sci-fi movies and electro-beams melting human skulls danced in my head as I left the table.

A few minutes later I returned with the bottle of Zinfandel and two decanters, vainly wishing the prep kitchen had a paint shaker so I might "put a little air" into the wine before serving it. Alas, it was not to be. I double-decanted the wine at the table and then poured a taste for the host. He smiled broadly and gestured for me to pour for the others at the table. Just as I finished pouring his glass, the oysters showed up, and everyone tucked in ravenously.

A few minutes later, I checked back in to see how everyone was doing, more out of morbid curiosity than anything. I fully expected someone at the table to voice a complaint about the tannin-bivalve insurgency in process, but not a word. Instead, they ordered a second bottle of Death Star and another dozen oysters. Then, they ordered a third bottle just as the salmon and Petrale hit the table.

Conventional food and wine pairing wisdom said that they should have been suffering the cruel fate of horribly mismatched food and wine chemistry. But there was nothing of the kind. In fact, the two couples were, by all appearances having a grand time. They polished off the third bottle with dessert and coffee. Then the host palmed me $20 on the way out. He thanked me profusely, saying they hadn't seen their friends in a couple of years, and the fact that we had their favorite wine made the evening perfect. I stood in the wake of the front door as it closed, completely stunned. Even with my newly acquired MS pin, nothing had ever prepared me for what had just happened.

The lesson I took from the "Death Star incident," as it came to be known, was simple: always give someone permission to enjoy what-ever they like to drink, regardless of how much you know—or, in this case, think you know. Otherwise, in doing what you believe is the right thing, everyone loses. And context, as in "this is my favorite wine," trumps everything.

I'd like a Fernet Branca, please.

8-22-12

31

LET THE SOMMELIER HELP

One of the more memorable sommelier experiences at Cypress Club happened early one Saturday evening. I was working the shift that night with the late Randy Goodman, a good friend and fellow sommelier. It was early on, and a party of four had just been seated on the main floor. The two couples at the party were clearly friends and looking forward to sharing a night out. I immediately noted that one of the guys was carrying a magnum of red wine, which he placed in the middle of the table with a flourish. No doubt he would attempt to impress-bore-torture his wife and friends with the wine. One more important detail. His wife was sitting across from him. And she was wearing a white linen dress.

The stage has now been set.

I approached the table, said hello, and offered the bottle owner's assistance with opening and serving the magnum. The wine turned out to be a current release of a popular Napa Valley Cabernet. I gently reminded him that there would be a corkage fee on the bottle. He said corkage was not a problem and that he didn't need help. Further, he had things under control and would take care of opening and pouring the bottle for his wife and friends. I nodded and returned quickly, placing glassware and an under-liner for the bottle on the table. I again offered to open the wine for him. Bottle guy responded, saying he had everything under control. I clearly remember him using that phrase twice.

I then ambled over to the other side of the restaurant and stood next to Randy, who had watched the initial exchange with great interest. He turned to me and said, "This is going to be rich." What happened next can only be described as the worst-case scenario.

Bottle guy retrieved a fancy corkscrew from his pocket. First, he stripped the magnum of its capsule, demolishing it in the process. He then turned the bottle on its side as he inserted the auger of the corkscrew. Next, with enthusiasm not unlike a Jehovah's Witness approaching the first doorstep of the day, the bottle guy quickly removed the cork from the bottle. Following, he removed the cork from the auger of the corkscrew and placed it in the middle of the table so everyone could be as impressed as he was. Then, with what can only be called deadly intent, he grabbed the magnum by the bottom of the bottle with his right hand to pour the wine.

I have to stop for a moment and note that pouring wine using this grip —holding the bottom of the bottle—is problematic at best, especially with a magnum. Unless you have huge Dwayne Johnson hands, the likelihood of sloppy pouring, drips on the table, or other more tragic mishaps always looms. Moving on.

Bottle guy went to pour for his wife and guests. What happened next can only be described as catastrophic. As he reached across to pour for his wife, she of the white linen dress, bottle guy lost control of the magnum and dropped the bottle on the table right in front of her. Wine immediately started sloshing out of the bottle onto the table and glugging relentlessly into her lap.

As the bottle hit the table, every head in the restaurant whipped around to see what was going on. Service came to a screeching halt. Instantly, Randy and I were across the room at the table. I grabbed the bottle, put my hand over the top, and set it upright on the table. Randy—and two other bussers who had appeared at the table out of nowhere—immediately started triage, cleaning up the table with cloth napkins. They also helped the poor woman sop up what must have been at least six ounces of bright purple Cabernet that had made its way into her lap.

The incident happened so quickly that she was stunned and could barely move, much less breathe. Bottle guy was also frozen. The other couple was horrified. With Randy and the bussers' help, cleanup was quick. I then offered the four diners a glass of Champagne at the bar while we reset the table. After several awkward seconds, the other couple said something like, "Why don't you give us a few moments." We did, retreating a safe distance away to await further instructions.

The four of them sat in stony silence for about a minute. Suddenly, bottle guy's wife stood up and forcibly threw her napkin in his face. Then she grabbed her purse and stormed out of the restaurant. The other couple watched in shock as she left. They spent the next couple of minutes staring at the flatware. Then they looked at each other, stood up, wished their friend Godspeed, and left. Bottle guy sat in stunned silence, looking at the comet trail of Cabernet that now adorned a goodly portion of the tabletop. I walked up quietly, put the cork back in the bottle, and handed it to him. Then I said, "We got this." He nodded, got up, and left the restaurant.

As the curtains of the front door billowed with bottle guy's hasty retreat, dining in the restaurant resumed but with a great buzz over what had just happened. The cleanup and reset of the table took longer than usual. The rest of the evening went without incident.

After the shift, Randy and I were downstairs having a Fernet Branca in our office. We replayed the accident multiple times, poring over every detail. We pondered bottle guy's fate and whether he would be sleeping on the couch--or in the garage--and for how long. We also wondered if his wife would hound him in the future every time he went to open a bottle of wine, especially in front of friends. Would she forever remind him of the "incident," and rightly so? In the end, we agreed that the matter was simple. If the sommelier offers to help, let them. And don't be a pain.

5-19-20

32

TERROIR REDEFINED

One night at the Cypress Club, I was assigned to work a party in the private dining room. The guests comprised three families with little kids who were staying at a nearby hotel. The kid part was unusual because the restaurant was known as a night spot. Regardless, even though the party wasn't in the main dining room, it was only a matter of time before all the kiddies were underfoot, getting in the way of everyone trying to work the table.

As dessert was served, one of the guys in the party called me over and said they wanted one more bottle of red wine. Something special. I brought over the list. He looked it over for several minutes and then chose an older vintage of Cabernet from a noted Howell Mountain producer. I confirmed the order, then went downstairs and retrieved the bottle from the cellar. Then I set up new glassware for everyone, brought the bottle to the table, and presented it.

At this point, I noticed the little girl who was the daughter of the guy who had ordered the bottle. She was climbing all over his lap and, frankly, being a nuisance. She had also been pest numeral uno for the entire evening; the one kid in the group who was always right in the way when you were trying to pour wine, clear glasses or dishes, or just get around the table. I also noticed that she was wearing pink slip-on jellies, or plastic shoes. My daughter Maria, who was four at the time, also had a pair and often wore them. The shoes would soon come into play.

After presenting the bottle, I decanted it per usual protocol at a side table within sight of the guy who ordered it. I then placed the bottle on an under-liner in front of him and quickly returned with the decanter. Just as I went to pour a taste for him, his daughter interrupted, saying, "Here, Daddy, taste the wine out of my shoe." Turns out she had taken off one of her pink jellies and was holding it out to him. In response, he looked at her, looked at her little slimy pink plastic shoe, and said, "OK, honey." He then took the shoe from her and held it out to me. What followed in the space-time continuum was like the scene in the movie *Dodgeball*, when the team from Ordinary Joe's comes out on the court wearing BDSM gear. Then the referee looks at them and says, "OK."

In my role as sommelier, it was my charge to take care of the guests and not bias their experience with my opinions. Given that, I simply smiled, nodded, and poured a splash of the wine into the proffered pink jelly. Dad made a big theatrical show out of swirling the shoe, somehow not spilling. Then he smelled the wine (it must have been god-awful) and took a sip. He smiled, turned to his daughter, and said, "It's delicious!" Then he motioned for me to pour for the rest of the table. I did just that, keeping a wary eye out for the now besmirched jelly to see what would happen to it. It went right back on the kid's foot. I should have known. Meanwhile, the conversation at the table went right on without pause.

In the weeks to come, the incident became known as "jelly terroir" among the staff at the restaurant. I wonder if the guy remembers it. As for his daughter, she's probably married now with her own kids. And I wonder if she even remembers it. I know I do.

5-18-20

33

MY EPIC SOMMELIER FAIL

This tragic story unfolded early one Saturday evening at Cypress Club. A couple was seated early on in one of the deuce booths against the far wall. I let them settle in for a few minutes and then approached the table, offering to assist with the wine list. The guy, a dapperly dressed older gentleman, asked for a few moments. I nodded and obliged.

When I returned to the table some minutes later, the man looked up, handed me the list, and said without hesitation, "We'll have the '76 La Tâche." I didn't see that coming. I hesitated for a long moment before responding with something along the lines of, "Great choice. I'll get that right away for you."

Let's pause for a moment for some background on the wine and an important sommelier strategy. First, the wine. La Tâche is one of the top Grand Cru red Burgundies from the venerable Aubert du Villaine of Domaine de La Romanée Conti. It's also one of the most expensive wines on the planet. At the time, the '76 vintage was hundreds of dollars on the list. However, the wine was Burgundy and, therefore, subject to vintage inconsistency that has historically defined the region, especially in the 70s. The 1976 vintage in the Cote d'Or region was a warmer, very dry year. Wines from the vintage that I had previously tasted were an odd combination of dried/stewed fruit, weedy character, and somewhat astringent on the palate. The La Tâche was no exception—although it was still an utterly superb wine.

One more thing about the wine and experiencing older Burgundy in general. By the time the owner of the restaurant purchased the case at auction, the wine was already 15 years old and heading into maturity, especially given the character of the vintage. With that, the '76 would initially show off aromas after being opened for at least the first 10-15 minutes. Then these off-aromas would dissipate, and the wine would be glorious. Any experienced sommelier, wine professional, or collector would know this. Which brings us to an important sommelier strategy--and where I failed.

Whenever someone orders an expensive older wine, the sommelier absolutely must perform an instantaneous and accurate assessment of the guest in terms of judging their experience with the bottle they've just ordered. Do they know what they're getting? Do they have previous experience that will enable them to enjoy the wine? These two questions—and more—flashed through my head in the instant just after the guy ordered the bottle. However, given the way he ordered the wine—with certainty and congruence—I made a snap decision that he knew what he was getting. And I hoped I was right.

I wasn't.

I quickly returned to the table with glassware and an under-liner. Then a second trip with the bottle and a serviette. I presented the bottle and began to tell him about the times I had tasted the wine, describing it in detail. Mind you, I should have done this very thing when he ordered the wine. But I didn't. Regardless, I proceeded to open the bottle, place the cork on the under-liner, wipe the top of the bottle thoroughly, and then pour him a taste. He smelled the wine and immediately frowned, saying the wine was bad. "Pour some for my wife and see what she thinks," he said. I did so and she reacted the same way. "Oh, this is really bad," she said.

In an instant, I knew I'd made a monumental mistake. The dapper older gentleman was clueless about Burgundy, much less older Burgundy. Immediately, I went into triage mode, talking about the glorious complexities of older Burgundy and how, most of the time, one had to wait at least 10-15 minutes for off-aromas from bottle aging to dissipate. Then the wine would be something truly special. I suggested we pour a bit in both their glasses and then let it sit while they perused the menu. Then, I'd return after a short time, and we would reassess the wine. He grudgingly agreed but said that he didn't see how time could possibly change a bad wine.

After ten long minutes, I approached the table and asked them to re-taste the wine. They did so with the same reaction. I sighed, apologized, and said I would be more than happy to remove the wine and glasses from the table. I then suggested that we take a look at the list to make another selection. He agreed, and I cleared the glassware and bottle to a nearby side station. Then I returned with the list. He asked for time to look at it.

When I returned to the table, he handed me the list with authority once again and ordered... a current release of non-vintage sparkling wine from Sonoma County. I'm sure I registered some surprise and then repeated the order to make sure I'd heard him correctly. He repeated it. I nodded and walked away from the table feeling like a complete rube. Like I'd been had.

Several things then had to happen in short order. First, I had to serve the bottle of sparkling wine. Then I had to figure out what to do with the now open bottle of La Tâche that would not last forever. I quickly went back to the table with sparkling wine service accoutrement: bucket, stand, under-liners, and serviettes. In moments, I returned with the bottle, opened it, and served it to them. They were happy; God bless them. Then I consulted with Randy, who mentioned that the sous chef would be coming in for dinner with his wife later in the evening.

It was their anniversary. We quickly agreed they would be drinking the La Tâche—after we both enjoyed a good splash of it.

I continued to give the couple great service throughout the meal despite the fact that part of me wanted to set a pack of rabid Dachshunds on them. C'est la vie. However, there is one more strange twist to this story. As I approached the table to clear the bucket and stand at the end of the meal, I saw the man scraping the rest of his entrée—fish of some kind—into a Ziploc bag. There was another Ziploc bag hanging half out of the breast pocket of his blazer. I stopped, stunned, and looked at him. He looked back at me, realizing he'd been caught, so to speak. Our eyes locked for a brief moment. Then I shook my head, and cleared the bucket and stand.

What did it all mean? Why did the guy order the La Tâche to begin with? He clearly didn't have a clue about the wine. Was it some kind of show for his wife? Was he a serial expensive wine bouncer? Whatever the case, in the end, the dark and murky cloud had a shiny silver lining. The sous chef and his wife enjoyed the bottle of La Tâche for their anniversary dinner. They said it was the best wine they had ever tasted. As for Ziploc Guy, he and his wife were never seen at the restaurant again.

5-24-20

PART SIX

NOTES FROM THE ROAD

To an outsider, a wine trip seems like a dream junket where we, the anointed industry professionals, are escorted in luxury from winery to winery in some foreign exotic locale. There, we're treated like royalty by winery owners and importers as we taste (drink) our way through zillions of expensive wines and eat at fabulous restaurants.

In reality, wine tours are a different animal. More often than not, the trips are like death marches where you and a group of people in the trade you probably don't know (but will soon know all too well) are stuck in a van for hours a day for a week or more. The daily schedule of appointments can be brutal, with four or five stops a day and between 60-100 wines tasted.

Hopefully, the food will be decent. Many times, it's not. Because wine is involved with every meal save breakfast, there's entirely too much protein and little in the way of green. There was a time when vegetarians perished on one of these trips. Now it's better, but vegans are still in the same boat. Traveling in Spain or Italy, and you're a vegan? Good luck. Otherwise, part VI of the book is filled with various adventures I've had over the years on wine trips.

34

MY FIRST DURIAN
EXPERIENCE

In February of 2013, I was in Singapore teaching a Master Sommelier class. At some point near the end of dinner one night, fellow MS Brian Julyan and I suddenly thought we smelled natural gas in the restaurant where we were dining (or mercaptan, to be precise, which is added to natural gas to make it detectable). The odor was strong enough that we called a server over to let them know about it. He answered quickly, "No gas, just durian." The phrase had barely left his mouth when another server put down a plate of white pastries in front of us. Brian looked at me and tersely said, "No way." After all, he'd been burned once before and had never forgiven me for it. "I'm going in," I announced to the table. I then took one of the spongy pastries off the plate and quickly popped it into my mouth without further thought. What followed was an instant descent into a wormhole of culinary/sensory hell with the most bizarre combination of horrific aromas I've ever experienced.

This wasn't my first encounter with durian. In 2006, I went to Singapore for the first time with Brian and Evan Goldstein to teach the inaugural MS Introductory Course in Asia. As we headed out to dinner one night, we drove past a produce stand on the side of the street that had an enormous stockpile of bizarre-looking green fruit. Someone in our party asked Tommy Lam, our local contact, about the fruit, which resembled a cross between a green football and an armadillo. "Durian," he said. "Tastes good but smells really awful." Being the ever-curious and compulsive Americans, we had to know more. After all, how bad could something possibly smell? Tommy drove around the block to satisfy our morbid curiosity and then rolled down the windows on our second pass. Instantly, a stench assaulted the car--a combination of fecal, road kill, and the essence of the putrefaction-decay cycle. It was overwhelming. That people would even consider eating something that smelled so foul was beyond belief. But I still had to know more.

The name durian comes from the Malay word "duri," which translates as thorn. In Asia, it's called the "king of fruits." Durian is known for its large size (up to 12 inches long) and can weigh up to seven pounds. There are some 30 known species, of which nine produce edible fruit. More than anything, durian is legendary for its remarkably strong, repulsive odor—an odor so pungent that it's banned on public transportation throughout Southeast Asia. Otherwise, durian has been consumed since prehistoric times but has only been known to the western world for about 600 years. The earliest known European written record of the fruit is by Niccolò Da Conti, who traveled to Asia in the 15th century.

I asked students in that first Introductory Class about durian and whether they liked it or not. The group was split right down the middle, with half crooning at the mention of the word and the other half utterly repulsed. There was no middle ground. Those who loved it professed to be addicted to it. One young woman said she considered durian to be an aphrodisiac or, at the very least, a delicacy. She went on to say that the combination of sweet melon-like fruit with jalapeno-pepper spiciness was to die for. Meanwhile, someone else in the class said it should be completely outlawed. Several in the group also said that eating too much durian in a short period of time could cause dangerously high blood pressure. I imagine one's olfactory bulb would probably explode long before that.

After that initial drive-by experience, Brian, Evan, and I teased each other for days about trying durian. But it wasn't until the very last day of the trip in the basement of one of the city's well-known shopping mega-complexes that we had our opportunity. Wandering through the glaring fluorescent-lit aisles, Brian and I came face to face with a kiosk called "Durian for All Seasons." We looked at each other, knowing that if we were ever going to taste durian, this would be it. As fate—either fortuitous or cruel—would have it, next to the register was a plate filled with samples of small wafer cookies with a thin green filling. "Come on, Brian," I said, "how bad could it be?" Note to self. Anytime someone asks that question, the answer will be some variation of *as bad as possible*.

I took two of the cookies and handed one to a reluctant Brian. As I popped the cookie into my mouth, I experienced something that's happened every time I've tried durian. It's like slowing down or even stopping time. Allow me to explain. Whenever I've tasted durian, I'm reminded of the time when I was a kid riding my bike on a hot summer day, and I wiped out on a neighborhood street that had just been repaved. Just as I was about to hit the pavement, time slowed down and almost stopped. I could smell the tar of the new pavement, feel the heat coming off it, and then feel myself hitting it and bouncing a few times--all in super slow motion. Eating durian was similar, probably because the olfactory experience is so overwhelming that it short-circuits the part of the brain that tracks time.

After eating my cookie, I looked at Brian. His expression was somewhere between stunned and mortified. He looked back at me and said with quiet desperation, "Coffee! Now!" We raced up four endless escalators to a coffee shop and waited ten long minutes to be seated while the taste of green radioactivity bubbled away on our palates. After an eternity, we were seated and immediately ordered. Brian didn't speak for a long time. Finally, after he finished a second cup of strong black coffee, he turned to me and said, "You, sir, have betrayed my trust." I don't think he's ever forgiven me for it.

Back to that night's dinner. As I popped the durian pastry into my mouth, I was assaulted by that unique durian stench and experienced time stopping once again. Gearoid Devaney, the third MS in our trio, described my expression as "like someone being electrocuted." I sat quietly, managing the sensory overload as best I could while the conversation at the table and the din of the restaurant went on around me. The experience was reminiscent of having a natural gas line installed in your mouth. I reached for water several times and also downed my glass of the most tannic red wine on the table. The stench and taste diminished after a few minutes but were still there in force long after. They would remain for hours, with the last remnants still there the next morning after repeated brushing and flossing. But I would survive to tell the tale.

What wine pairs well with durian? It probably doesn't exist. Much stronger water is needed, and only something in the spirit's world could possibly match the intensity. I'm not curious enough at this point to do any further research. As for your own durian adventures, you have been warned.

3-7-13

35

BEWARE THE ANGRY
PHILISTINES

It was April of 2001 and my second trip to Germany. I had been there the year before with the same importer. During that first trip my group spent over a week traversing through most of the country's wine regions, visiting as many as four wineries a day. Lest you think a trip like this is a picnic, let me point out that tasting over 400 young high-acid Rieslings in eight days is utterly brutal on one's teeth and gums. After returning, I had to reschedule getting my teeth cleaned for a couple of months. Otherwise, my dentist—and dental hygienist— would have been appalled. The scolding would have been legendary. There's nothing like dental shaming.

The trip started with three days in the Mosel, surely one of the most gorgeous wine places on the planet. The valley looks like someone decided to plant a section of the Grand Canyon with grape vines almost two millennia ago. The producers we visited in the Mosel were all-stars, including the likes of Mönchhof, Wegeler, Dr. F. Weins-Prüm, J.J. Prüm, Fritz Haag, Schloss Lieser, and Reinhold Haart in Piesport.

At every stop, we were tasting the 2000 vintage which had just been bottled. We also had the opportunity to taste a lot of older wines, which was wonderful.

After our time in the Mosel, we drove for several hours to Iphofen in Franken, traditionally called Franconia. Our one-stop in the region was at the Hans Wirsching winery. While the Mosel is the epicenter of Riesling, in Franken, the Sylvaner grape is king. Few, if any, do Sylvaner better in Germany than Wirsching, much less anywhere else.

A note about Sylvaner. More often than not, the grape (sometimes spelled Silvaner) is about as thrilling as a Toyota Camry. In other words, it gets you places, but no one's life is changed. This is not so when it comes to the Wirsching wines. Their top Grosses Gewächs Sylvaners from the Iphofer Julius-Echter-Berg and Iphofer Kronsberg vineyards are among the finest wines made from the grape anywhere.

After tasting the entire range of stellar Wirsching wines from the new vintage, we went next door for lunch. The meal was set up in a long, wood-paneled room. The walls were filled with various trophies of small game animals that had met a sudden and tragic fate by being in the wrong place at the wrong time.

Lunch consisted of a theme and variations on "vitamin P"—pork. Platters of sausages of every shape and kind, some resembling Dr. Seuss creations, were passed. After I piled my plate high in an assortment of wurst, I asked the woman serving us for some mustard. She didn't speak English, so I quickly turned to the son of the importer to translate. He rattled off something in German to her. She first stared in disbelief at him—and then me—before quickly turning on her heels and striding back into the kitchen. After many long minutes, she returned with a small, ancient metal can of powdered mustard. She then made a huge gesture out of showing me the can before sharply whacking it down on the table in front of me. I paused, thinking that if I asked for anything else, my head would quickly join the others displayed on the room's walls.

I was stunned. What was a kitchen in Germany without real mustard? I was also in a quandary. I had to use the mustard for the sake of appearances if not survival. Using a table knife, I managed to pry the small lid off the top of the can and then scooped a mound of the yellow-brown powder onto my plate. For the record, it looked like rust from an old pipe. Then, using the skills of a four-year-old first encountering broccoli, I moved the mustard around my plate after eating the delectable sausages. Problem solved and international incident avoided.

Fast-forward to the end of the trip. On the second to the last day, we were in the Pfalz region, just across the Rhein from Alsace. The Pfalz, formerly the Rheinpfalz or the Palatinate, is one of the sunniest and warmest regions in Germany. The wines of the Pfalz, especially the Rieslings in both dry and sweet versions, are opulent, powerful, and utterly delicious. As for history, some two thousand years ago, the Romans conquered the area to take advantage of its thriving agriculture and strategic geographical location on an important trade route. I mention this because the entire region is strewn with Roman ruins and artifacts. I remember our car pulling up to a stop sign on a country road at one point and looking over to see a stone sarcophagus in someone's front yard that had probably been there for the better part of 2,000 years.

Lunch that day was in the town of Bad Durkheim at a famous restaurant called Dürkheimer Fass. Why famous? Because the restaurant is located in what is believed to be the world's largest wine barrel. It's nearly 50 feet in diameter and, if filled with wine, would hold almost 550,000 gallons. In other words, it's a really big-ass barrel.

Victuals involved another huge plate of sausages (when in Rome) along with real honest-to-God Wiener Schnitzel. The latter was tender and juicy with a light, crispy crust slathered in an artery-stopping cream sauce. No wonder so many of the older patrons seated at the tables around us were shaped like smaller versions of the restaurant.

On being served my plate of sausages, I once again pined for mustard. After the previous episode, I was hesitant about asking for anything. But I mustered the courage (ha!) and asked our waitress, who spoke perfect English, if I could have some mustard. She immediately smiled and said, "Of course." Within seconds, she returned not with an ancient tin of caustic powder but a large tray filled with jars of locally produced mustard. It goes without saying that I was beside myself with condiment bliss.

I thanked her profusely and then told her about my experience at Wirsching. She listened intently, her frown growing and her eyes narrowing the longer the story went on. When I finished the tale, she stared at the floor for a long moment and then looked up at me, hissing the phrase, *"filthy barbarians."*

Later that afternoon, in the car, I thought about her response. In the olden days, the mustard provocation at Wirsching could easily have ignited an incident. If the exchange had happened with nobles around the table, it could have been deadly. Someone's face would have been roundly struck with a heavy glove and a challenge issued. Chairs would have been pushed back violently and a medieval version of the Jets and Sharks would have ensued sans dancing and a snappy Leonard Bernstein soundtrack.

In the end, food regionalism—even of the mustard kind--runs deep. I think about sweet tea in the American South, what passes for chile in any other part of the U.S. outside of New Mexico, and the vast and mysterious universe of BBQ. Whatever the case, there's just one thing. Never, ever screw around with mustard.

9-18-21

36

ATTACK OF THE LIVER CHICKEN

On a cold, damp, and foggy night, five of my fellow UK MS examiners and I were crammed into one of those charming, proper, and bone-rattling London cabs. Our destination was Motcombs, a restaurant off Sloane Street, a stone's throw from Harrods. With a full bar upstairs and dining room below street level, the place could easily be set in a '50s film noir, given the low wood-beamed ceilings, prints of celebrities on the walls, and the odd romantic deuce here and there. But what really makes the restaurant so unique, especially in the late fall, is the menu. It's game season.

Between 2006 and 2010, I had the privilege and pleasure of helping with the Master Sommelier Diploma exam in London four times. Over the years, the U.K. exam has been a smaller event compared to those in the U.S. At the time; the London exam was given on consecutive days at two of the city's finest hotels, the Capital and the world-famous Dorchester. The theory exam was held on day one at the Capital. The tasting and service exams were at the Dorchester the next day, with a reception and dinner following at the hotel. But dinner the first night was traditionally held at Motcombs.

This was my fourth dinner at Motcombs, and the only difference was the conspicuous absence of the legendary Val Brown. Percival Brown has been a mainstay of the London wine and spirits industry for the last 60-plus years. His career began in the 1950s and he is without a doubt among the who's who of the London trade. Val's energy is boundless, and his jokes are pointed and innumerable. But Val's presence also meant several mystery bottles to be tasted blind before the meal. The bottles were victims of a flood in one of his cellars, a flood that deprived all the bottles of their labels. Practically all the wine in this particular cellar was Bordeaux from the 50s and 60s. It was then up to us, members of the examining team, to divine the vintage, commune, and--if possible—the chateaux behind the mystery bottles.

Having little experience with tasting claret from the 60s, I have to say that the wines were striking, but not for the reasons one would imagine. In style, the wines from Val's cellar were about as far away from today's Bordeaux as possible. Without exception, they showed a depth of color somewhere between aged Reserva Rioja and Grand Cru Burgundy. Moreover, bottles such as 1963 Château Gruaud-Larose, 1966 Château Lynch-Bages, and 1960 Château Léoville-Barton were medium-bodied wines at best but elegant, refined, autumnal, and very complex. For the record, I never had much luck identifying the wines, but fellow U.K. Master Sommeliers Brian Julyan and Brian Dawes were usually spot-on with identifying vintages, communes, and some-times even the chateaux.

However, on this particular night, Val Brown had a previous engage-ment that couldn't be broken. So, we raised a glass in his honor and then set about examining the menu for dinner. Past meals at the restau-rant provided me the opportunity to try several different game birds. But tonight, the only game listed on the menu was the gamiest of them all—grouse. I had it several years previously on my first visit to the restaurant and remember it as clearly as tasting my first Fernet Branca. The two have a lot in common in that they're considerably bitter. I'm not sure why this feathery little friend has such a strong, liverish flavor. Perhaps it's like other denizens of the animal kingdom in that, upon the moment of death, it releases various chemical substances into its bloodstream as a final and defiant *screw you* gesture to the universe at large. However, fellow MS Nigel Wilkinson informed us of the fact that most grouse are now domestically raised, only to be released just before the fall season.

Whatever the case, I was not about to pass up the opportunity to partake. I did so and ordered the bird done medium. Not long after appetizers and Champagne were enjoyed, my roasted friend appeared on a massive oval plate perched atop a large piece of toast. The waiter offered several sides to accompany the fowl, including a rich gravy, a white gelatinous substance that turned out to be suet, and fine roasted bread crumbs. I opted for just the gravy. A large slab of bacon was draped over the top of the bird, offering a salt and fat counterpoint to the impending gamey bitterness. Then I tucked in and relished one of the great epicurean traditions of the fall season. And life was good.

3-7-14

37

EL PONCHO PERDIDO (THE LOST PONCHO)

There was a time in the early 70s when the gaucho look was all the rage in women's fashion. Suddenly, suburbs were afloat in bolero hats, leather boots, and gaucho pants, which always looked to me like bloomers that had somehow lost their bungee. I seem to recall my Mom having a poncho as part of this style, too. Her poncho had tassels and a belt. Eventually, the gaucho look went the way of hot pants, platform shoes, and the safari look. Little did I know it would later boomerang back into my life decades later in a very curious way.

Fast forward to December 2019, when I spent five days in Chile under the auspices of Wines of Chile, the country's wine PR and trade association. The invite came from my good friend and fellow MS, Evan Goldstein. The trek down involved two flights: first from Burque Flats (Albuquerque) to Houston. Then an overnight connection to Santiago, which took nine hours. After landing, going through immigration, and retrieving my bag, it was time to meet up with the tour.

The group comprised 25 wine professionals from throughout the U.S., including several MS colleagues. After an hour-long bus ride, we were ensconced in a faux-modern hotel outside of Santiago, next to a grand 19th-century estate called Las Majadas. A picnic lunch on a spacious lawn underneath giant trees was followed by the first tasting of the trip, conducted in the ballroom of the manor house. Introductions were made and the trip's agenda was explained in detail. Then, the group tasted more than 50 wines, covering a broad range of styles and accompanied by discussions moderated by winemakers.

Dinner that night was at the Las Majadas restaurant. The wine theme for the evening was Carménère. If not familiar, Carménère is a red grape/wine that does especially well in Chile vs. other locales around the globe. Originally from Bordeaux, Carménère is also a member of the Cabernet Sauvignon family. Other siblings include Cabernet Sauvignon, Merlot, Cabernet Franc, Malbec, and Petite Verdot. Though they're six different grapes/wines, one aspect manages to rule them all, to find them, and in the darkness bind them. It's a chemical compound called pyrazines. The term may sound exotic, but its associated aroma and flavor is commonplace. Pyrazines smell and taste like green bell peppers and herbs. And Carménère is known as being the most pyrazenic member of the Cabernet tribe.

To liven up the pre-dinner festivities, the trip's organizers thought it would be a splendid idea to have a tasting contest of sorts. In short order, I, along with two other MS colleagues, was drafted and paraded in front of the entire group. The goal of the contest was to taste two Carménères blind and try to identify them from a list of wines tasted earlier that afternoon. The prize for winning the contest was a real-life, honest-to-God poncho (pictured above) made from the wool of native sheep from the island of Castro. Said island would be our destination the next day after a short commuter flight. The rest of the trip would be spent there doing tastings, excursions, and more.

The climate of Castro, being located fairly south in the Southern Hemi-sphere, is similar to Seattle or Vancouver. It's lush and green because it rains--a lot. And it's cold. I can only imagine the poor sheep that contributed their fleece to the prize poncho as well as other woolen goods the island is known for.

Back to the contest. We were given five minutes of final Jeopardy time before having to reveal our choices for the two wines in front of God, colleagues, and a deaf universe. Fortunately, I had my notebook containing notes from that afternoon's tasting. Unfortunately, my two colleagues didn't have their notes.

I tasted the two wines, using my notes as a reference. The first wine was elegant and restrained for Carménère but still had the herbal/veg-etal stamp of pyrazines. I immediately pegged it as the wine from a winemaker I'd met earlier in the day. The other entry was more along the lines of a Carménère frat party. It was huge, inky dark in color, and had ripe, almost raisinated fruit. The weed garden thing was still there, but it was like a noisy kegger was also in progress. After consulting my notes, I quickly chose one of two wines from the afternoon tasting that I thought were similar in style.

In no time, the five minutes were up. Neither of my colleagues were able to ID the two wines. I got the first wine right, but not the second— and I won the contest. General hoopla ensued. After all, it was the first night of the trip, and no one was hungover or sleep-deprived. Yet.

Then, with great flourish, the trip organizers took the prize poncho off its pedestal and tried to bestow it upon me.

Several things then occurred to me in rapid succession. First, the poncho was heavy, almost to the point of being like the lead vest they put on you at the dental office when they're going to take multiple X-rays of your skull, not to mention irradiate your person. Second, the wool was incredibly scratchy. Wearing the prize poncho for even brief periods of time would be an exercise in masochism, not unlike the penitents of old who wore mohair shirts and flagellated themselves before the cross. But as bad as the heavy-scratchy parts were, it was the third factor that was the deal breaker. The wool of my newly won prize was corked to the extreme. So corked, it would have shamed well water. The TCA was like a force field. I literally recoiled as two winery reps tried to put the gaucho-con serape on me. I immediately turned to the group, who were all busy taking photos on their phones, and announced that the poncho was hopelessly corked. High hilarity and mayhem ensued.

No surprise, I refused to wear the corked poncho. After some quick negotiations, we settled for displaying it on a chair in the front of the room but at a considerable distance from all the diners. That didn't stop many of the attendees from coming up to check out how corked it was, like little kids passing around a carton of curdled milk.

After massive quantities of roasted cow and Carménère were consumed, the trip's organizers made welcome speeches. Then we headed back to our hotel rooms in the dark, me with the hopelessly corked poncho in tow. As I carried the stinky and heavy pile of wool, I was troubled. What the hell would I do with it for the rest of the trip? There was no way on earth I was putting the thing in my suitcase. First, it wouldn't fit. Second, even if it did, I could never suffer lugging the thing around for the duration, knowing it would permanently contaminate all of my belongings, not to mention the suitcase.

A solution presented itself the next morning. After we got to the airport, I sought out one of the trip's organizers and asked if he could mail the poncho back to me in the States. He immediately said yes, and took the offending gaucho garment and my business card, saying he would personally see to it after the conclusion of the trip.

Thankfully, it didn't happen. The Wines of Chile guy never got around to mailing it. I'm glad he failed in his mission. Had the poncho actually shown up, I would have taken it to Goodwill within 24 hours. Otherwise, somewhere in Santiago, a forgotten poncho now lies in darkness, collecting dust and becoming more corked every day. But at least it's not in my garage. And that's a very good thing.

1-21-22

38

THE PERILS OF SHOWERING
ON THE ROAD

One of the unexpected challenges of traveling over the years is having to deal with countless hotel room showers. Other than remembering the room number—something I've forgotten more times than you would believe, the single most important thing I had to figure out about a new hotel room was how the shower worked. Odds are I wouldn't be using it until early the next morning. But it was imperative to figure out how all the strange dials and knobs in the shower worked before I actually had to use them.

I could go on a rant at this point about hotel room design—especially hotel bathroom design. Some seem to have been planned by evil toddlers or chimps, with the toilet strategically placed so that the bathroom door won't close. But it was usually the shower that defied logic and reason. More often than not, the fixtures controlling water and temperature required several minutes to decipher. I have to once again note that the mysteries of shower operation had to be solved before actually using the shower. That's because I was always running behind in the wee morning hours trying to get ready for the day's class or event. I simply didn't have spare minutes to stand there naked as a wee babby trying to figure out how the shower worked.

Beyond the garden variety hotel room showers, there were experiences in foreign climes. Combine jet lag with science fiction bathroom design and you have the makings for experiences unusual and bizarre, not to mention embarrassment and abject humiliation. For your edification and amusement, here are two of my finest shower moments in exotic locales.

APRIL 2008 – SINGAPORE: HELLO SENTOSA

Our contact in Singapore met me at baggage claim at the immaculately spotless and beautifully designed Changi International Airport. The MS Intro Course and Certified Exam that year were being held at a new and very swank yacht club called ONE°15 Marina. It was so named because it was literally one degree south of the equator. The club was on Sentosa Island across the bay from City Center. To say that it was exclusive was an understatement. The weekend we were teaching coincided with the resort hosting an annual sale of Ferraris and Lamborghinis that were fashionably parked on the lawn facing the harbor. No surprise that Singapore's young and upwardly mobile were there in force, inspecting the uber-expensive wheels.

Our contact got me checked in, and then I headed back to the airport to pick up my colleague, who would soon be arriving. I went up to my room on the second floor and found it was large and immaculately appointed. One entire wall was floor-to-ceiling windows that looked out over the marina and across the bay to the City Center skyline. The view was magnificent. However, the room was also one of those high-tech affairs where a touchscreen tablet controlled everything from lights to curtains and beyond. In my addled state, the buttons seemed like they were labeled in Sanskrit. Keep in mind that I'd been on a plane for the better part of the previous 24 hours. At least I figured out how to open the drapes and how to turn on a few lights.

After unpacking, a shower seemed like the perfect thing. It goes without saying that the bathroom was also a marvel of design and technology. The large bathtub/shower zone was sunken below floor level and featured benches, cup holders, and a dazzling array of nozzles, shower heads, and dials. It also had another touchscreen tablet built into the wall just as you stepped down.

I undressed and got into the shower. In my fragile state—and having no patience whatsoever--I started randomly pushing buttons on the tablet with the hopes of simply turning on the water and getting cleaned up after the long trip. The result was the stuff of high comedy. Water came blasting out from multiple sources at both extreme hot and cold temperatures. I squawked and cursed a few times before finally getting the water to a manageable temperature. I then went about my business of tidying up.

It was at some point during the final rinse cycle when I turned around to see the marina below and the gorgeous skyline in the distance. Moments later, I also realized that at least a half dozen people who had just been looking at very expensive cars were now staring up at me. A young child holding his mother's hand was pointing at me, no doubt saying something like, "Mommy, why is that man naked up there?"

The realization that I was doing the personal hygiene thing in front of an unknown audience hit home with a force stronger than the jet lag I was feeling. I immediately knelt on the floor and reached up, pushing any number of buttons as I desperately tried to figure out how to close the blinds. Instead, I was rewarded with random blasts of ice-cold and scalding water at varying velocities. I finally crawled out of the shower and found the "all off" button on the touch screen. Then I dried off out of sight next to the expensive toilet that also had an array of buttons and special features.

When I woke up from a nap a couple of hours later, I made myself a double espresso with the in-room Nespresso machine. Then I spent the better part of 20 minutes figuring out the tablet at the side of the bed and the one in the shower. Fortunately, there were no complaints to hotel management about the guy in room 215.

SEPTEMBER 2008 - JEREZ, SPAIN: THE ELEPHANT CAR WASH

This story took place later the same year in a very different place. I was part of a group of industry people touring and tasting in Sherry country. A quick side note to say that Sherry is the most completely misunderstood wine on planet Earth. Especially in the U.S., where the traditional idea of Sherry was long thought to be sipping multiple tiny glasses of Harvey's Bristol Cream. Otherwise, everything about the wine, from the styles (most dry), how to serve it, the right glassware, or food pairing, is an unknown quantity. To the last point, Sherry is one of the greatest food wines there is.

Getting to Jerez from San Francisco involved three flights: San Francisco to Newark, Newark to Madrid, and Madrid to Jerez. A brief mention of the last flight and our approach to the tiny Jerez airport. The pilot, who no doubt had a military career, made the steepest bank in a commercial jet I've ever experienced. The plane almost turned on its side as we made our final approach. The rest of the passengers, mostly commuter types, paid no heed whatsoever. I almost soiled myself. Had I not been wearing a seat belt, it would have been like the part of 2001: A Space Odyssey when Frank Poole gets blasted into the airlock without a helmet.

After meeting up with the group, we bussed it over to our accommodations. I was assigned a fully furnished two-bedroom apartment. It was large, spacious, and beautifully appointed, with lots of local artwork. The bathroom was equally grandiose. The shower was enormous—the biggest shower I have ever seen outside of a gym. You and at least 10 of your closest friends could easily have shared a splashy without crowding. The glass walls of the palatial stall were also covered in a labyrinth of polished copper pipes and fixtures.

In my once again jetlagged state, I disrobed, stood inside the shower, and tried in vain to figure out the maze of dials and knobs. After many moments, I said, "screw it," and went for it. What followed has become known as the Elephant car wash incident. After turning the first couple of dials, I was blasted from all sides by ice-cold water. It was as if someone had turned several fire hoses on an unexpectant— and quite naked—victim. I squawked mightily and jumped back out of the huge stall, swearing and sputtering. Water continued to blast from several of the shiny copper shower heads. I shook off the immediate trauma and then snaked my way back into the stall, trying to avoid the jets of ice-cold water. After an infinity of fumbling with dials and knobs, I managed to turn off all the water. Then minutes of mindless experimentation followed, with me cold and dripping wet the entire time. Finally, I was able to turn on one of the many faucets and get the water hot. I then showered quickly, expecting the threatening array of pipes to betray me at any moment.

For the record, I never figured out the elephant car wash. I simply used the one dial I knew would get me clean without another traumatic incident. It was like owning a Formula One car and driving it around the block in first gear at 15 mph. But at least I was safe. And I was clean.

4-3-21

39

FEAR AND LOATHING ON THE WINE TRAIL

One of the aspects of wine trips that's rarely mentioned is the drivers—those who ferry your wine group to vineyards and producers. They can be consummate pros or ordinary hacks who somehow got roped into driving your group around for the day or a week. The young Greek lad who drove our group around his country for ten days in September of 2006 comes to mind. He wore the same polyester disco shirt the entire trip. I tried not to get close to him after the first couple of days. I'm sure he just stood the shirt up in his hotel room at night. And he definitely redefined the term "terroir." Yes, car experiences on wine trips can sometimes be the stuff of legend, and they can also be some of the most terrifying moments in one's life. Here are four personal fear and loathing experiences on the wine trail.

MARCH 2000: ACONCAGUA, CHILE

At the time, I was working for the artist formerly known as the original wine.com. The trip was billed as a "Sommelier Summit" for a group of august U.S. wine professionals. We were shown wineries and vine-yards near Santiago and Casablanca for several days. On the last day of the tour, I opted out of sightseeing with the group to instead go to a small winery in the Aconcagua, located about 90 minutes from where we were staying. My assignment was to taste through their inventory and choose some selections to directly import for wine.com.

I was picked up promptly at 8:00 AM by a young goateed lad in a smallish Euro car. I piled into the front seat and immediately noticed two things: first, the floor was littered with trash and fast-food wrap-pers. Second, there was a small plastic statuette of the virgin attached to the dashboard. Little did I know I'd be praying to the tiny icon in a matter of minutes.

The goateed lad immediately took off from the hotel at ramming speed into traffic. In no time, we were on the highway, which wasn't actually a highway but a two-lane affair with a middle passing lane. My driver immediately started to pass any car or truck he could. I quickly discovered the gestalt of highway driving in Chile. Your single mission was to go as fast as you could and pass every vehicle in front of you to do just that. Using your blinker to change lanes was less than optional. But there's more. All the other drivers were trying to do the same, including those in the opposite lane. This meant that the middle lane became a dangerous DMZ of sorts in which a never-ending game of chicken was played, with the bigger vehicle or driver having the largest cojones winning brief and perilous stand-offs.

Within minutes, I was gripping the handrest with one hand and the seat with the other and repeatedly stomping on an imaginary brake pedal, which was in reality, a pile of trash. I must have told goatee man that we weren't in a hurry at least a dozen times. He nodded every time and then stepped on the gas. At some point during the first hour, I had the sudden realization that my life was in the young man's hands. And if the gods were willing for us to live to see another day, so it would be. If not, at least the end would be quick. But it would also be messy.

In time, we made it to the winery which was in the foothills of the 20,000-foot Mt. Aconcagua. It turns out that the goateed lad was one of the owner's sons. The latter took me through the winery, which was not much more than a concrete and corrugated metal building filled with tanks and barrels. Then we sat at a table and tasted over 20 wines. I made notes and chose six of the samples. We then discussed pricing and logistics for getting the wines to California. After a quick lunch, it was time for the return trip to the hotel, which was just as harrowing. But I don't remember most of it because I slept—or pretended to.

APRIL 2006: DOURO, PORTUGAL

I was in Portugal with friend and fellow MS, Keith Goldston, under the auspices of the cork producer AMORIM. For the better part of a week, we had been touring cork forests, cork production plants, and a few wineries. Towards the end of the trip, we drove from Porto to the Douro Valley about two hours away. The Douro is one of the oldest vineyard areas in Europe. It's also a barren landscape resembling the Grand Canyon, with vines planted on steep, craggy hillsides that rise hundreds of feet from the river. Dynamite is actually used at times to put in new vineyards. The climate is also extreme, with temps averaging over a hundred degrees Fahrenheit during the summer. Fortunately, we were there in March before the heat set in.

Our driver for the week was the lovely Maria Rosita. She was bubbly, charming, and talked a mile-a-second. Maria was perpetually on her flip phone (remember, this was 2006) giving trip updates to her boss or chatting with friends. Maria also drove fast. Insanely fast. We must have made the trip between Lisbon and Porto in record time.

Our first appointment in the Douro lasted until late afternoon when it began to rain. Keith and I piled into the back of the rental with Maria at the wheel. Our destination was the hotel-restaurant for the night. In no time, it was dark and pouring. Once settled behind the wheel, Maria rolled her window down (deluge and all), lit a cigarette, and then put on a cassette (yes, a cassette) of the Rolling Stones full blast. She had already told us multiple times that they were her favorite band. Maria then called one of her best friends to talk about the soccer game the night before between Porto—her team—and a close rival.

From there, things went like this. It's pitch dark and raining in sheets. From my window, I can see the lights of buildings on the banks of the river hundreds of feet below. The town of Pinhão, our destination, is blinking in the distance. Maria is driving as fast as the tiny single-lane road—now shiny and slick--will allow. There are wickedly sharp switchbacks and hairpin turns at regular intervals, but they're not well-marked. Meanwhile, Maria yells into her phone and waves the cigarette out the window with her other hand. I'm not sure how the car is being steered. With each turn, Keith and I are tossed against each other or against our door. But the finishing touch is the music. "You Can't Always Get What You Want" is blaring from the fuzzy warbles sound system. The song has never been the same for me. It never will be.

APRIL 2006: DOURO, PORTUGAL

Same trip the next day. In the morning, we toured Quinta do Crasto, a Port producer. After lunch, Maria dropped us off at Niepoort, a historic family-owned house specializing in aged Tawny Ports and dry wines from Port varieties. Dirk Niepoort is one of Portugal's most important winemakers. He's also an affable, no-nonsense guy. After introductions, we piled into his Land Rover for the trip up a very steep hill—as in, a 40-plus-percent grade—to the winery. The Land Rover was ancient, one of those thick, rattly metal cans with an engine and drivetrain that are good for nothing other than traversing off-road or up really steep hills at a snail's pace.

I got in the front seat next to Dirk. Keith and the rep from the PR company were in the back. I immediately noticed there were no seat belts and mentioned it to Dirk. He looked at me as if I had two heads. "Why would you need them here?" he asked. I shrugged. We then chugged in slow motion up the bumpy dirt road to the top.

Just as we reached the summit, Dirk suddenly said, "damn, I left the keys down at the house." At this point, anyone else would have slowly turned the car around to go back downhill. But not Dirk. With left hand on the steering wheel, he clanked the mighty Land Rover into reverse. Then he turned around to look backward and told us, "You'd better hold on." What followed was 30 or more of the longest, scariest-ass seconds of my life. Any wrong move with the steering wheel, however slight, and we would have somersaulted hundreds of feet to the bottom of the vineyard. We might even have made the river. Someone in the back yipped at one point. I just held on to anything I could for dear life. After an eternity, we reached the bottom of the road and zipped up to the side door of the house. Then Dirk looked at me and said, "What?"

MAY 2008: PALERMO, SICILY

Flying into Palermo from Rome took all of 35 minutes. Unfortunately, my suitcase did not make it. Trying to make sense of that with the woman handling missing luggage was hit or miss at best. But I did show her my passport and the name of the hotel, so there was a glimmer of hope.

Afterward, I met up with a colleague, and we grabbed a cab to the hotel. The cabbie nailed every stereotype of his ilk possible. He was large, unkempt, and given to laying on the horn, waving his fist, and screaming at any car that wasn't going fast enough. And this was even before we got out of the parking lot. Once we got on the freeway, he hit his stride. The good news was that the hotel was only 30 minutes from the airport.

By the time we got into Palermo, it was rush hour. No surprise that the cabbie became even more incensed by stopped traffic, muttering and periodically leaning out his window to abuse some random driver who then did likewise. When in Palermo…. But scary cab driver had one more trick up his sleeve. At some point, he made a sharp left turn down a major one-way street at some point—going the wrong way. Cabbie guy took the far-right lane, lowered his head, laid on the horn, and drove. Cars and trucks coming towards us scattered like pigeons on a playground, some ending up on the sidewalk.

I had one of those moments described in the Chile incident above. There was nothing I could do, and it was only a matter of seconds before this crazy moron got us all killed. But it didn't happen. Instead, he whipped a hard right turn and screeched to a halt in front of our hotel. Before we could even move, he was out of the car, the trunk opened, and my colleague's suitcase was tossed in front of the bell stand. We got out, and he immediately demanded to be paid. "Basta!" he said with his hand out. I paid him and he got back in the cab, muttering and giving me the eye. But there was a happy ending to the story. My suitcase turned up around midnight. And I had lived to be able to open it.

1-14-22

40

ME AND ASHURNASIRPAL

Tom Standage's "History of the World in Six Glasses" is a good read.
Standage writes for *The Economist* and has published several books.

This is by far my favorite. The book frames history from the Stone Age to the 21st century through each of the era's signature beverages–beer, wine, spirits, coffee, tea, and Coca-Cola. Standage charts the history of each and shows how certain beverages influenced historical movements and even entire civilizations. For example, how the workers in ancient Egypt relied on a diet of beer and bread to build the pyramids. Or how one of Washington's first official acts in 1794 was to send a militia of over 10,000 men to Pennsylvania to put down a rebellion over whiskey taxes. And how the tea industry in China was inexorably linked to the opium trade. Then there's wine.

Standage writes that wine appeared later than beer by thousands of years. He then highlights what has to be one of the largest and most excessive celebrations in human history hosted by one Ashurnasirpal II, the king of Assyria from 883 to 859 BCE. During his reign, Ashurnasirpal II embarked on a huge plan of territorial expansion, conquering lands to the north and west, even exacting tribute from the Phoenicians on the Mediterranean coast. By all accounts, his methods were brutal. After conquering the Aramaeans and Neo-Hittites in what is now modern Syria, his armies put down a two-day revolt. Then he had a monument raised in his honor with the following inscribed:

"Their men, young and old, I took prisoners. Of some, I cut off their feet and hands; of others, I cut off the ears, noses, and lips; of the young men's ears, I made a heap; of the old men's heads, I made a minaret. I exposed their heads as a trophy in front of their city. The male children and the female children I burned in flames; the city I destroyed and consumed with fire."

Yes, Ashurnasirpal II was a cruel rat bastard of the highest order. But the man also knew how to throw a party. Standage writes that the feast held to celebrate the building of the new Assyrian capital in Nimrud lasted for ten days. Over 70,000 attended and were served 1,000 fattened cattle, 1,000 calves, 10,000 sheep, 1,000 spring lambs, 500 gazelles, 1,000 ducks, 1,000 geese, 20,000 doves, 12,000 other small birds, 10,000 fish, and 10,000 jerboa—a kind of small rodent. Vegetables, if you're curious, were an afterthought, with just 1,000 cases served. Astounding as the previous list is, the most important part of the festivities was the fact that wine—not beer—was featured. No doubt beer was the common beverage at the time, having been extant for at least two millennia. But wine was a prohibitively expensive rarity, produced hundreds of miles away in mountain vineyards. It had to be transported downriver to the new capital by boat. In serving wine, the king demonstrated his power and wealth to all his subjects and beyond.

After finishing the book, I forgot about Ashurnasirpal II until one cold fall day in London in 2008 when I was in the UK to help with the MS exam. I flew in early to have a museum day, spending the morning at the Victoria & Albert, one of my favorite museums anywhere. After lunch, I took the underground to the British Museum. It was my first visit there and initial impressions can only be described as "over-whelm." In a rare moment of common sense, I booked a tour. I'm glad I did. Our guide was named Emma. She was thin as a reed and about 5'5" with wire-rim spectacles and graying hair done up in a bun so tight she'd never need plastic surgery. Emma's voice was a bit on the shrill side. It reminded me of Frau Greta Farbissina in the Austin Powers movies in that she shouted out directions, often startling those in our group as well as innocent bystanders.

Our first stop on the tour was the Rosetta Stone, one of the most remarkable artifacts from the ancient world. Emma warned us there would be a huge crowd and that it was imperative to stay close together and follow her instructions. Then, from at least 30 feet away, she slowly backed up toward the exhibit, with our group following close behind. Those already viewing the Rosetta Stone had no choice but to move as our group moved forward. Several people complained about being pushed aside. One Italian guy even yelled at us. Frau Farbissina barked at them in response, telling them to go elsewhere. And they did.

Once in front of the exhibit, Emma gave us a thorough rundown of the stone and explained why it's so important to the history of language.

Finally, after the crowds threatened to go all wonky around us, we took off for calmer locations. Our next stop was at the Elgin Marbles. When someone in the group asked her about the possibility of the museum returning the marbles to the Greek government, she responded with something like, "That will happen when hell freezes over." Otherwise, the tour lasted about 90 minutes and was more than worth the price of admission. At the end, I tipped Emma five pounds, more than anything, because I was scared of her. But she actually smiled and thanked me.

Afterward, I had tea and a snack at the café in the Grand Court with its roof of 3,312 individual panels of glass held together by four miles of steel (!). Then I spent at least two more hours in the museum, going from end to end, mind agog the entire time as I looked at the exhibits. Before heading out, I strolled through the antiquities one last time. At one point, I rounded a corner to find an enormous room with the walls covered in ancient Assyrian stone reliefs. As I scanned the scenes, I suddenly stopped cold. In the middle of one of the reliefs, there was a kingly sort holding a cylix—a shallow bowl for wine. He was undoubtedly fresh from having just slain a giant beast or two. Suddenly, I realized who he was. It was my buddy, Ashurnasirpal II.

In seconds, I became verklempt, even a touch misty-eyed. Maybe it was the jet lag. Whatever the case, I knew it was him. I thought about this mighty but evil ruler from the ancient past who deigned to serve wine to his subjects. And how, in a way, King Cruel Shoes was responsible for my career. I silently thanked him but immediately cursed him for his utter contempt for human life. Regardless, it was a moment. Just me and Ashurnasirpal. And then the moment passed. But not before thinking about what kind of wine would pair best with small rodents.

6-20-22

PART SEVEN
HUMOR

As much as I've enjoyed my career, I've never failed to see the humor in wine culture--and for good reason. The industry has always been an easy target. The precious factor alone guarantees never-ending fodder for jokes and hyperbole. The last part of the book looks at the quirky and often absurd aspects of wine for the sake of humor. Sometimes, it's all you need.

41

FLYING DONKEYS AND MAL VINO

Carla and I have shared a bottle of wine with dinner practically every night for the better part of the last thirty-plus years. It's rare that we don't finish a bottle. On the odd occasion that we don't, it's usually because there's a time constraint on dinner, which happens infrequently these days at the compound. Otherwise, it means mal vino, as in something wrong with the wine. That happened the other night when we didn't make it through a bottle of Morgon, a Cru Beaujolais.

To go all wine geek on you for a moment, in the last ten years or so, certain producers in Beaujolais have elevated their game to new heights. Thanks to various importers and the press, notoriety and recognition for these producers and their wines from the ten Crus—top appellations—have increased significantly. Not surprisingly, so have the prices, which have more than doubled in some cases. But I think it's justified. These winemakers, and others in their respective Crus, have been making superb wines for decades and were unjustly overlooked and underpriced.

Also worth noting is the fact that some of the producers make wine without fining, filtration, or added sulfur. All are worthy aspirations with the caveat that the juice in the bottle has to be microbiologically stable. That's because whenever you send a bottle sans soufre (without sulfur) out into the world, bad things can potentially happen. In the case of our bottle, the culprit was Brettanomyces, a type of yeast that originates in the vineyard and ends up in the winery environment and ultimately the wine.

The presence of Brett in wine, as it is called, is highly contextual. In small amounts, it can add a richer texture, earthiness, and some complexity to a wine. However, too much Brett and the dark side appears. Then it makes itself known in the form of fecal, barnyard, and small rodents covered in Band Aids. There's one more thing about Brett. Human tolerance for it is highly individual. Some actually like the smell and taste of Brett, while others loathe it even in trace amounts.

Back to dinner the other night, which featured cheeseburgers from the grill and a salad. After setting the table, I retrieved the bottle of Morgon from the small 36-bottle wine fridge, which is next to the dining table. A wine fridge is mandatory here behind the adobe curtain because the climate is about as inhospitable for wine as it gets. It's either too hot or too cold, and it's too dry all the time.

Once the burgers were ready, I opened and poured the Morgon. Initially, the temp of the wine was on the chilly side—50 degrees, which is the setting on the fridge. It would soon warm up, much to its detriment. More on that in a moment.

After finishing the burgers, the conversation ranged from events of the day, which included our daughter Maria getting a new job with the University of North Carolina, her undergrad alma mater. We then chatted about other happenings. I mentioned a book I was reading by Italian physicist Carlo Rovelli. It's a collection of essays called "There Are Places in the World Where Rules Are Less Important Than Kindness." A long title, but a good read.

I own all of Rovelli's books. He's a brilliant physicist and one of the best in his respective field. He's also a superb writer, able to explain hifalutin theories like quantum mechanics and black holes. One of the chapters in his book touched on Einstein's theory of how time passes at different rates depending on multiple factors. I told Carla how Einstein proposed time passing more quickly, although minutely, at high altitude vs. sea level. Hence, people living at high altitudes age more quickly than those living at sea level. She looked at me skeptically the whole time with the Spock one raised eyebrow.

"That's the most ridiculous thing I've ever heard," she said after the fact. "You mean to tell me that time passes at different rates according to altitude?" I answered in the affirmative. "So, what about watches and other things that keep time? They don't change their function depending on the altitude." I had to agree. But I also had to remind her that I was just the messenger and not the author. Also, physicists after Einstein had confirmed his theory as being true.

Carla responded with a harumph, saying, "I reject Einstein's idea." Then she took a sip of wine, frowned, and put her glass down. "Does the wine taste weird to you?" I quickly smelled my glass and said that there was a lot of Brett. And as the wine warmed up in the glass, the Brett had really started to come out. Mind you, the wine was fine when I first opened it. But oxygen has a funny way of revealing any cosmetic flaw in a bottle.

I then tasted the wine and quickly confirmed what Carla had said. The Brett in the bottle was about to stage a coup and overwhelm the entire character of the wine. Think militant, marauding livestock. The wine was changing color, too, turning brownish right before our eyes.

"I'm not so sure I like this wine," Carla said. "Then you probably wouldn't like the part in the book about flying donkeys either," I said. "Flying donkeys?" she responded, giving the eyebrow a workout. "Yeah, there's a chapter in the book where Rovelli writes about the Australian philosopher David Lewis. He put forth the idea that there are an infinite number of parallel universes. That being the case, there is at least one alternate universe where donkeys can fly. Maybe more than one."

The idea of flying donkeys was too much for Carla. "I'm going to go finish my sudoku," she said, "and I'm having a gin. This wine is not good." I immediately put my nose in the glass and had to agree. The Brett palace coup was complete. The wine smelled like sweaty gravy and had turned a rosy brown in color. I even saw the color brown internally when I smelled it. On the palate it was redolent of beef broth, livestock, and bitter metallic.

After Carla left the table, I pondered Einstein's notion of time passing at different rates. And how the theory had been proven to be true by other physicists. Still, I thought it was a good idea to question new scientific findings. After all, that's what scientists do. And if our watches really do go tick-tock slower at sea level than at the top of the ski slope, we should know about it. At least somebody should be able to explain it better than I can. As for mal vino, once bottled, wine without added sulfur can be a crapshoot. Otherwise, I think Neil Young once said that Brett never sleeps. He was right. And microbes always bat last.

10-22-22

42

RANDOM WINE
ASSOCIATIONS

There's an episode of Spongebob SquarePants where Spongebob and his best friend, Patrick Starr, must somehow pass through the perfume section of a department store. Mind you, this makes no sense, given that the show takes place in Bikini Bottom, which happens to be underwater. But as they say, movies is magic. And anything is possible in cartoons. So, our favorite sponge buddy and Patrick had to make a quick and awkward trek while scores of perfume samples were being squirted at them. The trip is short but perilous, with the two almost overwhelmed with clouds of Lilies of the Valley and Eaux de Auntie's Unmentionables.

Whenever I think of this particular episode of Spongebob, I'm reminded of cheap Viognier. If unfamiliar, Viognier is a white grape and varietal wine. Historically, the best Viognier-based wines are from France's Northern Rhône Valley and can command high prices. However, the grape is now cultivated all over the planet. In some cases, it's farmed en masse, almost like table grapes. As you can imagine, the quality of wines made from the latter can be lacking, sometimes considerably.

Regardless of locale or price point, what all Viogniers have in common are floral qualities. They smell like flowers, as in rose, honeysuckle, narcissus, and more. These floral aromatics come from a chemical compound called terpenes, which can naturally be found in the Viognier grape as well as other fully aromatic grapes like Muscat and Gewürztraminer.

That's more information about white wines smelling like flowers than you ever wanted to know. But it's this very floral quality in inexpensive Viognier that reminds me of the SpongeBob episode. Not to mention the times I've passed a perfume counter in Walgreens and been assaulted by an overpowering cloud of screechy scents, only to scamper to another aisle and bounce off a force field of TCA emanating from a rack of belts and purses.

The SpongeBob-Viognier connection came to me one time when I was judging a big wine competition. On the morning of day two, the panel I was chairing was tasked with blind tasting over 50 current-release Viogniers priced under $15. In minutes, I was right there with Sponge-Bob, just trying to get past the perfume counter. But it got worse. By the end, it was like being stuck in a truck stop café that reeked of cheap perfume, bubblegum, and cigarettes.

Over the years, random wine associations like the SpongeBob episode have occurred to me from time to time. I'm not sure if my industry colleagues experience this likewise. But they must. Maybe they just don't talk about it. Regardless, my associations usually take the form of a simile or comparison between a certain wine and a completely unrelated thing.

These associations may be a result of my not getting to wine as a career until my thirties. Coming to wine after seven years of college down the drain studying music history and trumpet performance meant my sensory mainframe had already been programmed to all things auditory. And my hard drive already had an entire other field of endeavor installed with reams of information. So, unlike many other MS students who now typically average younger in age, I had a strong frame of reference in a completely unrelated field. This may explain why I sometimes create random associations with various wines. I may be wrong about this, but I think it's true. Regardless, here are a few of the other wine associations I've made over the years.

ZINFANDEL: FRAT PARTY IN A BOTTLE

To me, Zinfandel always has the potential to get out of control. Perhaps that's because clusters of Zinfandel grapes ripen unevenly, meaning there can be green-shot berries and raisins on the same bunch. Take the average of the two, and the alcohol can top 15% after fermentation. Hence the frat party thing. But maybe Zinfandel is also the perfect speed dating wine where the goal is to make a strong impression in three minutes without offending anyone and then vacate the premises immediately.

RED BURGUNDY: THE EXPENSIVE MAINTENANCE GIRLFRIEND/BOYFRIEND YOU CAN'T AFFORD

Top Grand Cru Burgundies are the most expensive wines by far. I just now looked on winesearcher.com, and a single bottle of the 2018 Romanée Conti from Domaine de la Romanée Conti will set you back a minimum of $9K a bottle. Price aside, expensive Burgundy, like a high-maintenance girlfriend/boyfriend, has the capacity to amaze every now and then, but also to monumentally disappoint more often than not. There's an old adage concerning Burgundy that says nine out of every ten bottles are disappointing, but the tenth bottle is so astounding that you empty the bank to buy another ten bottles. Then, at some point, your pockets are empty, and the boyfriend/girlfriend stops calling you.

CHÂTEAUNEUF DU PAPE: A PICNIC GONE WRONG

Many moons ago when I was studying for the tasting exams, I continually struggled with getting Châteauneuf du Pape and Gigondas. Both are blends from the Southern Rhône based on Grenache. The blend part of the equation should have been my clue from the get-go. Finally, one day after missing a call on a Châteauneuf for the umpteenth time, it occurred to me that the wine didn't taste like any one thing—as in, a single grape. Instead, it tasted like a blend. I know what you're thinking. Doy-yoy. The good news is that, from then on, I got the wine. And the picture of the wine, so to speak, that came to me that day was the following:

Imagine that you and your friends decide to go for a picnic and watch the sunset. You find a suitable spot, light a fire, and then spread out a blanket. Then various victuals, including roasted meats, smoked fish, tapenades, chutneys, and other condiments, are set out. Bottles of vino are opened and poured. You watch the sunset, and everyone is having a grand time as it gets dark. That is until a wild beast of some sort starts making a racket in the bushes nearby, which freezes the conversation instantly. The menacing, snarling noises keep growing louder as the beast gets closer. Suddenly, someone freaks out, gets up, and runs away. That sets the entire group off, which does likewise, running for the cars and then speeding away.

The next day, you return to clean up the mess. In your absence, the mysterious beast–and no doubt others--made a feast of your picnic. The blanket is bunched up and most of the food has been eaten. What wasn't is mixed together and smeared all over. The blanket smells like dried meat, tapenade, animals, and pepper—exactly like aged Châteauneuf or Gigondas. The idea became my "picture" for the wine. It's worked ever since.

BRUT ZERO CHAMPAGNE: PENITENT SOCIALITES

Other than using larger glasses for service and decanting bottles, the most puzzling recent trend concerning Champagne to me is brut zero wines. These non-dosage bubblies are bracingly acidic and bone dry. Personally, I find no pleasure in drinking them. And pleasure is what drinking Champagne should be all about. But brut zero Champagnes are all the rage with some of my younger compadres. They argue that the dosage, or addition of a tiny bit of sugar and wine just before the bottle is corked and labeled, can dilute the true expression of Champagne and its terroir. This, to me, is an ill-founded notion, given that Champagne as a wine is practically always a blend. Adjusting the sweetness level with the dosage is simply a technique to ensure the wine is balanced.

Every time I taste a non-dosage wine, I'm reminded of the once-popular trend of self-flagellation in the Catholic church. Where one would practice self-punishment through various means to atone for supposed sins in the eyes of the Almighty. Here, behind the adobe curtain, the Penitentes were historically a religious order known for their practice of self-flagellation, especially during Holy Week. Combine the self-flagellation thing with the idea that Champagne has long signified the good life and upper crust in society, and you have a unique mélange. Socialites wearing mohair sweaters instead of cashmere, and drinking bubbly that makes one suffer. But they say it's for your own good.

CHABLIS: DOMINATRIX WINE

My first ever serious wine tasting was in the summer of 1987. I was bartending at what was then Bentley's Seafood and Oyster Bar in the financial district of the City. At the time, I had started to collect wine and was reading as much as I could about it. No surprise, my base of knowledge was California wines. I had barely dipped my toe into the enormous lake that was European wines. But I was bound and determined to learn.

One afternoon on my way to work, I stopped at Singer & Foy, a now-defunct wine shop off Washington Square in North Beach, the City's Italian neighborhood. The tasting listed in their mailer that day was, if you can believe it, several recent vintages of Premier and Grand Cru Chablis from Domaine Francois Raveneau. This was long before the brilliant wines of Raveneau attained cult status and became all but unobtainable.

I walked into the shop, the only customer at the time, and was greeted by owner Steven Singer. I told him I wanted to taste the Raveneau, and he smiled knowingly as if I had just uttered a password and gained entrance into some kind of secret club. After sitting down, Steven set out ten glasses in front of me and began to pour wines from almost identical bottles replete with hard yellow wax capsules. The same yellow wax capsules knowingly loved and hated by sommeliers the world over because they're almost impossible--and messy--to remove. After that, he left me in silence with the wines and my notepad.

To this point, my experience of Chardonnay was limited to the New World, primarily California. I had never tasted a good, much less great, Chablis. But I clearly remember picking up the first glass only to be greeted with a series of aromas that were alien to me. Not much in the way of fruit compared to the California Chardonnays that I was used to. Then I tasted the wine. The experience was like a combination of loud feedback on a public PA system and eating several whole lemons in rapid succession. That first sip of what was the 1979 Montée de Tonnerre was like someone had plugged a home electric appliance into my palate (waffle iron), and flicked the juice on with the expected results.

Nothing remotely similar had ever come across my vinous radar. Here was a wine that was immensely powerful, bare-bones dry, and painfully acidic. In comparison, the Chardonnays of my previous experience were like going to a church social as a kid. Some of them had big hair, others wore lots of jewelry, while still others wore an alarming amount of perfume.

At that point, I put the glass down and looked at the other nine wines, realizing that I was really in for it. But being of very stubborn Irish stock, I took a deep breath and resolved to get through the flight, and to somehow make sense of it. I had, after all, paid my $15 (!).

Somewhere around the sixth or seventh glass, I had two of my first wine epiphanies in short order. First, it was possible to come across a wine that was perfectly well made but that you disliked or even loathed. Second, and more importantly, some wines simply don't care if you like them or not. It was precisely at this moment that I dubbed Chablis and the flight of Raveneau "dominatrix wines." The wines truly didn't care if I liked them or not. They were also completely unapologetic for their character. And they would definitely not be calling me in the morning.

The tasting at Singer & Foy permanently etched Chablis in my brain-pan. Going forward, I would never have a problem recognizing it in blind tastings. But it took a few years for me to actually like the wines. Now—and to show you how one's palate can completely change over time—it's one of my very favorite white wines. I relish the sour lemon, salty mineral, and bracing acidity. But I still wonder about Chablis. If it was a dominatrix, what would its name be? I know. I think it's Lola.

12-11-22

43

ANOTHER GLASS OF NEIL

What is it about cilantro that it can split a room full of strangers right down the middle, with some people liking it and the rest utterly hating it? The very mention of cilantro, even the thought of it, sends the latter camp into a tizzy. It's like the classic overreaction to bugs where the victim gets all ooged out, squeals, and waves their hands about in an alarming manner. OK, so I'm exaggerating. But not by much.

Carla is squarely in the *I can't stand cilantro* camp. Always has been. Although there have been rare times when a drive-by experience with cilantro was tolerated and almost/nearly/sort of liked. Like in a salad dressing at a certain café in the City near where we lived. But the dressing also had avocado, other herbs, and plenty of lime. In other words, any number of things to take the "antro" out of cilantro.

A few months ago, Carla requested some fresh Italian parsley for dinner prep. Not the garden variety regular parsley, which has less than zero flavor. In fact, if you were to substitute plastic for regular parsley as a food garnish, no one would know. No one except for the rubes who insist on eating it. I hear it's good for your teeth. Italian parsley, on the other hand, actually has flavor and texture. When minced, it adds a lovely zing to any recipe as well as an attractive dash of green.

At the market, I strolled down the produce aisle and suddenly had to duck when one of the fake thunderstorms went off, sending a mist spraying over all the veggies. Once the mini-monsoon was over, I made quick work of grabbing a few carrots, some celery, and the afore-mentioned Italian parsley. And it was here, dear readers, that I failed. In my rush, I neglected to notice that the Italian parsley was parked just next to the cilantro. With barely a glance, I grabbed a bunch of the latter and tucked it, dripping wet from the recent deluge, into a plastic produce bag. Then I finished up my shopping.

Once home, I unpacked the groceries. Carla immediately noticed the cilantro. "What is this?" she cried, her brows all furrowed. "Uhhh... parsley?" I replied hopefully. "IT'S CILANTRO!" She didn't actually say it in all caps. But she did look at me as if I was a cat that had just shat the bathmat. Rhyming, it's a beautiful thing we all should do more of. I think you get the drift. It goes without saying that the dash of zip and green intended for the evening's entrée had to be left out.

No surprise that cilantro found its way into the post-dinner conversa-tion. How it instantly repels a certain portion of the populace, how it's a culinary no-fly zone, a line that must never be crossed, and an herb that must not be named. It got me thinking about other things that can instantly appeal or repulse. Neil Young's voice immediately came to mind. No doubt there are a lot of singers who really can't sing. Bob Dylan, David Hasselhoff, and Rex Harrison all fit the bill. But I can tolerate them for various reasons.

Neil is different. For me, Neil's voice is beyond fingers on a chalk-board. After 10 seconds of a Neil song, I start to get a little twitchy. By the end of a Neil song, I've already pondered committing several felonies. And if, for whatever reason, someone were to keep playing an entire album of Neil's shrill and whiny crooning, I might act on those misguided impulses with entire empires quickly falling. Don't get me wrong. I would be the first to say that Neil is a brilliant songwriter, and he's had an amazing career. It's just that, to me, his voice sounds like a cat being slowly squeezed, the same cat that just shat the bath mat. And there's not even any cilantro involved.

Neil's voice makes me realize that there are times in life when your parents' admonitions of playing nice, being fair, and giving everyone a chance simply don't work. When everyone is not going to get a gold star, a pat on the back, or a hearty "way to go." In short, there will be times when you strongly dislike something, and that's all there is to it.

Perhaps I'd make an exception if Neil was a kind of wine. Yes, that might work. Then there would be alcohol involved to offset the pressed cat thing. After one glass, Neil would almost be tolerable. After two glasses, Neil would start to sound like Maria Callas, and things would be rosy. If that's the case, I think we need some more Neil. Darling, could you please pass the bottle? I'd like another glass.

8-18-21

44

THE EVOLUTION OF A PALATE

"A man loves the meat in his youth that he cannot endure in his age."

— SHAKESPEARE FROM *TWELFTH NIGHT*

Some years ago, I interviewed Yosh Han, an internationally known custom perfumer. Like previous interviews with wine industry colleagues, I wanted to deconstruct Yosh's internal strategies for olfactory memory given that the range of possible aromas for perfume is exponentially greater than wine. I wasn't surprised to discover that Yosh's strategies for remembering aromas were entirely based on visual, and also similar to those of most of the wine professionals I'd interviewed.

During a second session, Yosh helped me create my own personal scent. We started with more than 50 vials of different aromas. Over several rounds, I narrowed down my favorites to just seven: peppermint, rosemary, violet, waves (marine note), aloe, night queen (jasmine), teak, and something called washed suede. Yosh then blended them and tweaked the percentages until we both liked the results. The final scent, at least according to Carla who knows infinitely more about perfumes and essential oils than I ever will, is a unisex scent that could be worn by either men or women. For the record, she likes it too.

Afterwards, I asked Yosh what aromas she liked best and which were her favorites. I wasn't surprised to hear her say that she likes practically everything so long as it's of high quality. She then asked me what kinds of wines I liked best. I had to give the same answer. I like practically any style of wine as long as it's balanced and well-made. But that hasn't always been the case. And that got me thinking about how my tastes in wine—my likes and dislikes—have changed over the last 30-plus years. It also made me ponder how one's palate undergoes an evolution of sorts over time. With that in mind, here's a completely unresearched, undocumented, and otherwise reckless account of the evolution of a palate.

WARNING: The following contains elements of sarcasm, droll humor, parody, and otherwise snarky commentary.

PHASE I: KATY PERRY

Wine as liquid confection. The wines from Phase I are slightly-to-moderately sweet in style. In the recent past we've had Muscat in all its various forms, as well as the category of sweet red wines. Both initially left the industry scratching its collective head while scrambling to get tanks filled and labels designed to be commercially appealing.

It seems as if every generation finds a way to give itself permission to drink fruity and slightly sweet wines. The Moscato/sweet red thing is no exception. That's because most of us, self-included, started in the way back machine of our wine careers by initially drinking wines that were off-dry to medium sweet, and hopefully balanced with enough acidity so as not to resemble, well … Katy Perry.

For me, those came in the form of Lancer's and Mateus rosés, odd vinous creatures called "wine coolers," and the likes of Blue Nun, Riunite Lambrusco, and White Zinfandel. Not surprisingly, most were mass-market brands produced by entities possessing the mega-funds to promote on TV and in print media. Don't get me wrong, everyone has to start somewhere. Ultimately though, one hopes that the Katy Perry crowd moves on to at least Phase II. But if they don't, it's all good. No harm, no foul.

PHASE II: SMOOTH JAZZ

Once upon a time, we had MUZAK, a style of music comprising perfectly played but completely bland renditions of popular showtunes and top 40 hits. One would hear MUZAK in elevators, at shopping malls, and in dental offices. Today, we have "Smooth Jazz," an idiom that once again features immaculate playing by top studio musicians performing a wide range of jazz-arranged tunes in state-of-the-art sound. We also have Smooth Jazz in the wine world: it's called Chardonnay, and it defines the second phase of palate evolution.

During Phase II, novice drinkers graduate from innocuous, sweet, and mono-chromatic wines to Chardonnay: a full-bodied single-varietal white wine with layers of intense fruit and the first taste of new oak, which will likely become the new drug of their personal wine world. Inhabitants of Phase II often become interested in what they're eating in terms of quality. This is despite the fact that they will consume mass quantities of Chardonnay with any and everything, including red meat. Eventually, many in the Phase II club will crave even more intensity and then discover red wines. Then, like every toddler boy who first learns to walk, they won't walk but will instead race full-bore, pell-mell, directly into …. Cabernet Sauvignon.

PHASE III: MONSTER TRUCK PULL

Having developed a serious oak habit, wine now becomes a full contact sport for newly minted members of Phase III. More often than not, it's a guy thing. No, make that a group of guys thing. As in a group of guys in the backyard having just consumed half a grilled steer and the better part of a case of very expensive Cabernet. Now they're moving on to cigars, Port, and the inevitable and emotionally awkward "I love you, man" moment.

For denizens of Phase III, a wine that doesn't have 15-plus percent alcohol is not wine. They tend to eat lots of red meat and often develop a serious fortified wine habit because, after all, Port is a really loud wine, too. Needless to say, the hangovers experienced by Phase III members can be legendary. The discovery of amaro (Italian bitters liqueur) is therefore common in this phase and often a medical necessity. I discovered Fernet Branca while in Phase III, and it saved my life on one such occasion. Alas, parenthood and advancing age can take their toll on members of Phase III. But a certain percentage of them experience a life-altering vinous moment at some point and move quietly into Phase IV.

PHASE IV: OH BLINDING LIGHT

During Phase IV, the wine drinker moves from full contact to nuance because of a beautiful-sadness-of-life moment, usually in the form of a great bottle of Burgundy. Instantly, wine goes from collision to filigree, and with this blinding light moment often comes the realization that the "where" of a wine can be more important than anything else. Such mystical moments sometimes occur while traveling to so-called sacred vinous environs such as Burgundy, Jerez, and the Mosel. Initiates of Phase IV also cross an invisible line from "eat to live" to "live to eat."

Planning dinner while having lunch is a common affliction. Potential downsides to Phase IV often involve becoming a hopeless and insufferable Francophile snob, with the victim never returning to a balanced vinous state. Extreme cases involve joining various wine societies or clubs that require secret handshakes, wearing pastel sashes with medals and ribbons, and even—God forbid—the donning of long Obi Wan-like robes. With their recent spiritual conversion, Phase IV rangers are notorious for demeaning big-ass Cabernets—the same big-ass Cabernets they were only recently hoovering at an alarming rate. Further, they may take to condemning any wine for having too much alcohol or for not being authentic, whatever that means.

PHASE V: IT'S A SMALL WORLD

Phase V is really an extension of Phase IV. Here, the individual has their first great Riesling experience, and with it, the blinding realization that wines with residual sugar can be cosmic—as great as any wines on the planet. Moreover, these same delicate, slightly sweet, and acid-crazy bottlings are among the most versatile food wines that exist. Phase V regulars often drink more white wines than red and crave what is, in reality, insane levels of minerality and acidity regardless of what's in the glass. But they also "get" simply made country wines with the right intensity of fruit and a good acid balance (that acid thing again). And if they haven't discovered Champagne and top-quality sparkling wines (think Franciacorta) in Phase IV, they do so with a vengeance in Phase V. Italy looms large for red wines in Phase V because of the acid/minerality thing. Oddly enough, Phase V'ers will put up with higher levels of VA and Brett to get their fix.

PHASE VI: EVEN THE IRISH

The title for this phase comes from the brilliant Mel Brooks movie *Blazing Saddles*, one of my three all-time favorite movies. Those who make it to Phase VI have traveled full circle in palate evolution in that they like practically every kind of wine as long as it's well made: from bone dry and austere VORS Palo Cortado Sherries to pyrazenic Coonawarra Cabernets, to VA-laced old school Barolo, to decadently succulent TBAs from Austria or Germany. Everything. As Mayor Olson Johnson of Rock Ridge once did say, "Aw, prairie s**t. Everybody!"

8-27-14

45

A MEAL FOR THE END
OF TIME

It happens every now and again. Someone will sound the alarm that the end of the world is nigh. That certain planets and stars have aligned, as predicted in some chapter in the Book of Revelations, signaling the end of time. Which will, of course, only come after great destruction and turmoil.

Reading these predictions about the end of the world always gives me pause. What if it's true? Not sure about you, but I wouldn't be pleased. But if the end was imminent and nothing could be done, one would probably experience the inevitable emotional boomerang of shock, outrage, despair, apathy, and then reluctant acceptance.

It goes without saying that one would have many intense *I love you man* conversations with friends and family. Soon, however, we might even find ourselves actually looking forward to the last 24 hours before the big show. Then there's the last meal. Now, that would be important. It's not to be confused with the last supper or one's last meal in prison. No, this particular last dinner would have to be spectacular seeing how it's literally the final meal before all of humanity and the creatures of earth go poof.

By the time dinner rolled around, one would undoubtedly have a ravenous appetite because, let's face it, one would never be this hungry again. However, with a universe of cuisines to choose from, confusion and paralysis could easily set in, what with the world ending and all. Focus would have to be the key. I personally would steer clear of any brash ethnic extravaganzas which might create digestive disturbances that would, let's face it, never happen. I'd also avoid any über-fancy Barbie food pageants of teeny tiny food on enormous plates, no matter the chef or the venue. Too much maintenance and too little time. Instead, I'd go for the jugular of gustatory experiences, the basic of basics, the urtext of fine dining. The menu would be as follows.

OYSTERS

I remember dining at an excellent seafood place in Singapore called "No Signboard." The restaurant is so named because there literally is no sign on the front of the restaurant. At the beginning of dinner, my tablemates tucked into the most gargantuan oysters I've ever seen (as big as a toaster). The very sight of these monstrous bivalves was, needless to say, unsettling. Eating oysters from and in a tropical climate is wrong. It's also violating the universal law of not eating anything bigger than your head. For me, the oysters have to be small, delicate, and with just a touch of brininess. Kumamotos are my favorite. Six, please.

Wine pairing

Champagne, of course. I'm a huge fan of blanc de blancs Champagne with oysters, so I'm thinking that a beautiful vintage of Salon or Krug Clos du Mesnil would be perfect.

CAESAR SALAD

Yes, I know the salad should follow the entrée. But it's the end of the world, so the rules de cuisine be damned. Here, I'm choosing romaine lettuce, the most abused member of the salad family that usually appears on the table as a mess of soppy greens slathered in a gloppy white substance, the content of which could be two molecules away from plastic. And the croutons are like leftover drywall. A well-made Caesar is my go-to salad and a thing of beauty. The romaine has to be fresh, vibrant, and crisp. The dressing has to be tart with more than a bit of citrus cut. The croutons have to be small and crunchy, and the cheese, a good parmesan. And don't hold back on the anchovies, please.

Wine pairing

We need an intense, mineral-driven, and bracingly acidic white here with no oak. A young vintage of Domaine Francois Raveneau Les Clos Chablis or Franz Künstler Hochheimer Hölle Grosses Gewächs sounds just right.

BACON

Why a bacon course? Because we can--and we should. After all, bacon is "vitamin P." It makes everything taste good. But we're not talking about any bacon here. Only serious bacon from a heritage breed of hogs like Berkshire will do and simply roasted. Jamón Ibérico would also do in a pinch. In fact, let's have both.

Wine pairing

A great vintage of DRC's La Tâche or Leroy's Le Musigny will do nicely.

STEAK FRITES

The ultimate entrée: a bone-in 24 to 26-ounce strip steak with an outrageous amount of marbling, such as Kobe beef done medium-rare over a very hot grill with a touch of charring on the exterior. The fries have to be twice-done in goose fat or duck fat and finished simply with sea salt and fresh cracked pepper. Perfection.

Wine pairing

There are too many great reds to choose from. I'd narrow it to three: a monumental vintage of Bordeaux ('45 Latour or '61 Cheval Blanc), California Cabernet ('74 Heitz Martha's Vineyard or Ridge Montebello), and an extraordinary vintage of Penfolds Grange or Henschke's Hill of Grace.

CHEESE

Once again, too many choices, so I'd narrow it down to just three favorites. They're like a trio of scandalous dwarves: Epoisses (stinky and runny), Stilton (salty and pungent), and a fine-aged Reggiano Parmigiano (crumbly and a bit corrupt).

Wine pairing

A trio of weapons-grade botrytis wines is the only solution here: great vintages of Yquem, Royal Tokaji Aszú Essencia, and Robert Weil's Kiedricher Gräfenberg Beerenauslese Goldkapsul.

POT DU CRÈME AU CHOCOLAT

With the end of the world literally just around the corner, the last morsel of food would fittingly be chocolate, one of mankind's greatest achievements. My only requirements here are that the chocolate has to be outrageously good and the texture of the pot de crème like weight-less wisps of silk.

Wine pairing

I'm going countercurrent here with a great younger vintage of Fonseca or Taylor's.

CODA

After dinner, we'd make our way to an arrangement of lawn chairs in the front yard. I'd pour myself a large Fernet Branca accompanied by a Montecristo No. 2.

Finally, the speakers would be moved from the living room to the front steps to play tunes for the end of time. What music would fill the air those last few precious minutes? Here are some initial thoughts:

1. "Stairway to Heaven," Led Zeppelin: NOT.
2. "It's the End of the World as We Know It," R.E.M.: Possible.
3. "Quartet for the End of Time," Olivier Messiaen: Good thinking, but it's too long and complicated.
4. Beethoven's Ode to Joy from the 9th Symphony: Gets my vote. It's a good tune, repeated several times, and everyone can join in or just hum if they don't know the words.

7-5-12

ACKNOWLEDGMENTS

During the years I intermittently worked on the book, a group of friends and colleagues read various drafts and provided pithy, wise, and sometimes blunt commentary. In my immediate tribe, thanks to Carla Peña-Gaiser, Maria Gaiser, and Melissa MacEachran, who read the first draft of every chapter. My siblings, Tina Wertz, Tom Gaiser, Anastasia Gaiser, and Terry Gaiser, also got a look at many of the chapters as they were written. Beyond that, a band of friends weighed in on various chapters as they were penned. In particular, I'd like to thank Michael Bugella, Liz Cooper, Mary Doan, Peter Granoff, Rudy Harper, Steve Jaqua, Ron Merlino, Bob Reyen, and Madeline Triffon.

A huge thank you to my daughter Maria, who did the major editing on the text. She's a superb writer and the best editor I've ever worked with.

Many thanks to my publisher Melissa G. Wilson at Networlding.com, who helped guide the book from manuscript to finished form. Melissa and Lynn Miller also took the book through its final editing phase.

Thank you to Robert Harrison for his outstanding coaching and guidance on finishing the book and beyond.

Thanks to Miladinka Milic of milagraphicartist.com for the cover design, and to Damian Jackson for the text formatting. The back cover photograph is by Kelly McCarthy.

Many thanks to my authors' group, which has been a wonderful resource over the last couple of years. In particular, thanks to James

Cogan, Patricia Garland, Diane Hopkins, Anne Janzer, Dawn Kristy, Alan Lake, Alastair McDermott, Lynn Miller, Irma Parone, Gerry Parran, Chip Scanlan, Robert Slayton, Joanne Telser-Frere, and Craig Wilson.

My appreciation and sincere thanks to the entire Master Sommelier community in the U.S. and the U.K./EU.

I also want to thank those who hired me at various jobs in the restaurant and wine industries over the years. In particular, thanks to Amy Albert, Doug Beiderbecke, John Cunin, Steve Goldberg, Peter Granoff, Kathleen Heitz, Bruce Minkiewicz, and Dennis Webster.

A big thank you to Christa Wojciechowski, who does a brilliant job with all my online publishing and social media.

A special thank you to good friend and colleague, Doug Frost. Doug is an outstanding educator, writer, and owner/winemaker at Echolands Winery in the Walla Walla Valley in Washington State. He's also one of five people in the world to ever pass both the Master Sommelier and Master of Wine examinations. It was Doug's company, "Strong Water LLC" that was the inspiration for the title of the book. Doug was kind enough to give me his blessing to use the phrase. I will always be grateful to him for that—and for his friendship.

Finally, deepest thanks and endless love to my wife Carla, daughter Maria, and son Patrick.

ABOUT THE AUTHOR

Tim Gaiser is an internationally renowned wine expert and lecturer. He is one of less than 300 individuals worldwide to ever attain the elite Master Sommelier title. He is the former Director of Education and Education chair for the Court of Master Sommeliers, Americas. Over his 30-plus year career, Tim has taught thousands of students in wines and spirits classes at every level as well as developing wine education programs for restaurants, winery schools and wine distributors. He has experience in all phases of the wine industry: online, wholesale, retail, winery, and restaurants.

Tim has written for a number of publications including Fine Cooking Magazine and the Somm Journal and also writes for numerous wine and spirits clients. He has served as the author and lead judge for the Best Young Sommelier Competition and the Top Somm Competition.

Tim's book *Message in the Bottle: A Guide to Tasting Wine*, published in 2022, has garnered outstanding reviews and is widely considered one of the top books on wine tasting for professionals, wine students, and consumers.

Prior to his wine career, Tim received an M.A. in Classical Music before developing his wine expertise. He played classical trumpet as a freelance professional and as an extra with the San Francisco Opera Orchestra. He currently lives with his family in New Mexico.

www.timgaiser.com

Newsletter sign up

www.timgaiser.com/blog

https://tgaiser.substack.com

Message in the Bottle

Printed in Great Britain
by Amazon